T0050030

"What a joy to soak in these illuminating ideas and engaging stories of how we each can live more fully and freely in our challenging times."

—Daniel J. Siegel, M.D., *New York Times* bestselling author of *IntraConnected* and executive director of the Mindsight Institute

"Sharon Salzberg's *Real Life* invites us to approach our one precious life with fullness and courage, without papering over the pain or the challenges."

—Angela W. Buchdahl, senior rabbi of Central Synagogue, New York City

"The jewel in the crown of the Real series. This gift of a book is filled with Sharon's signature style of blending keen observation, profound wisdom, and the easeful confidence of a trusted teacher."

—Amishi P. Jha, Ph.D, author of the national bestseller *Peak Mind*

"This book will put you in touch with your own deepest wisdom— and help you embody it in your own life."

—Scott Barry Kaufman, Ph.D., host of *The Psychology Podcast* and author of *Transcend*

"Sharon Salzberg is, above all, a master storyteller."

—Catherine Burns, artistic director of *The Moth*

"Sharon Salzberg shows us how to rebalance ourselves in the face of life's difficulties, and in so doing, free our minds and hearts to find bliss and wonder."

—David DeSteno, host of the podcast *How God Works*

"*Real Life* is far more than piercing, fierce instructions for cultivating lovingkindness as a means for our connection. It is also an elegy for the heartache of isolation and pathway to connection."

—Jerry Colonna, author *Reboot*

"Our great suffering is forgetting who we really are, forgetting the possibility for freedom in every moment. *Real Life* gives us a pathway of remembering. In this inspiring and powerful book we are invited to open to our full potential for wisdom and love, and offered clear, practical guidance for living from that basic goodness."
—Tara Brach, author of *Radical Acceptance* and *Radical Compassion*

"This book maps our life-giving journey from isolation to community, from confinement to freedom."
—Parker J. Palmer, author of *On the Brink of Everything*

"A shout of joy to welcome the hope-filled inner journey of this book!"
—Robert Thurman, professor emeritus of Columbia University and author of *Wisdom Is Bliss*

"Sharon has done it again; *Real Life* delivers another gem from the person I like to call the Queen of Loving Kindness."
—Atman Smith, coauthor of *Let Your Light Shine*

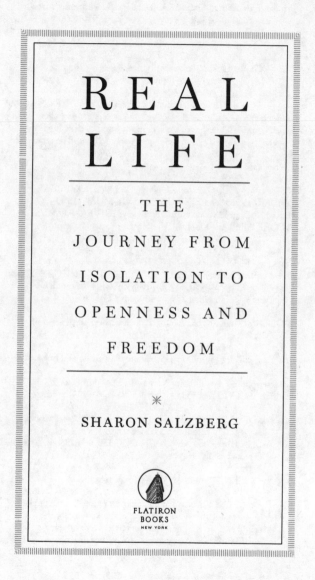

REAL
LIFE

THE
JOURNEY FROM
ISOLATION TO
OPENNESS AND
FREEDOM

✳

SHARON SALZBERG

FLATIRON
BOOKS
NEW YORK

www.flatironbooks.com

Grateful acknowledgment is made for permission to reproduce from the following:

Harvey Fierstein, for permission to reprint his interpretation of the saying "the last night in Jerusalem" from the virtual Saturday Night Seder, a collaborative effort to raise funds for the CDC Foundation COVID-19 Emergency Response Fund. The seder aired on saturdaynightseder.com on April 11, 2020.

"Louder Than Words" from *TICK, TICK . . . BOOM!* Words and Music by Jonathan Larson. Copyright © 1990 UNIVERSAL MUSIC CORP. and FINSTER & LUCY MUSIC LTD. CO. All Rights Controlled and Administered by UNIVERSAL MUSIC CORP. All Rights Reserved. Used by Permission. *Reprinted by Permission of Hal Leonard LLC.*

"Sunday - Finale" from *Sunday in the Park with George.* Words and Music by Stephen Sondheim © 1984 RILTING MUSIC, INC. All Rights Administered by WC MUSIC CORP. All Rights Reserved. Used by Permission. Reprinted by Permission of Hal Leonard LLC.

The Library of Congress has cataloged the hardcover edition as follows:

Names: Salzberg, Sharon, author.
Title: Real life : the journey from isolation to openness and freedom / Sharon Salzberg.
Description: First edition. | New York : Flatiron Books, 2023.
Identifiers: LCCN 2022035939 | ISBN 9781250835734 (hardcover) | ISBN 9781250835741 (ebook)
Subjects: LCSH: Self-actualization (Psychology) | Self-realization. | Mindfulness (Psychology)
Classification: LCC BF637.S4 S246 2023 | DDC 158.1—dc23/eng/20220812
LC record available at https://lccn.loc.gov/2022035939

ISBN 978-1-250-83575-8 (trade paperback)

Our books may be purchased in bulk for promotional, educational, or business use. Please contact your local bookseller or the Macmillan Corporate and Premium Sales Department at 1-800-221-7945, extension 5442, or by email at MacmillanSpecialMarkets@macmillan.com.

First Flatiron Books Paperback Edition: 2024

10 9 8 7 6 5 4 3 2 1

To all who journey toward freedom—
yesterday, today, and tomorrow

CONTENTS

✳

REAL LIFE

INTRODUCTION

❋

Embarking on a Journey Together

THERE ARE TIMES—and I suspect I speak for most of us when I say this—when we feel like we're merely bystanders to our own lives. There are times when we feel mired in habit, withdrawn and small. Even though we want to take a stand about something we care about ... we want to reach out to someone in need ... we want to go up to someone and thank them for their work, we are nonetheless suddenly seized by the conviction that our words or our actions couldn't possibly be meaningful, that we don't count as much as others do, that we should just shrink back and dwell in the long-occupied, constraining box we are accustomed to—so familiar, even if cramped and confining.

At the same time, we can also recognize those moments when even baby steps into new terrain are exciting, perhaps a little wobbly but also audacious, where we connect to something bigger than our fears and feel we are living more fully, learning and growing and having an adventure. When our trying new approaches or different behaviors does not feel destined to an imminent, sputtering end because of our belief that we're fundamentally limited.

Instead, possibilities abound.

Perhaps our early conditioning has trained us to imagine that very little happiness is available to us. An oppressive personal or cultural atmosphere might work to depict our right to joy as negligible, our room to move as awfully limited. A path to liberation counteracts this conditioning and culturally reinforced constriction. To accomplish such a transformation, it asks us to go forward into the full range of our feelings and reactions with kindness and honesty. When we do so, we realize that we can travel from painful constriction to expansion and freedom.

This is not a one-and-done journey. It's something we repeat again and again, not because of compulsion or obligation but because we are fueled by the happiness of discovery, by the relief of openness, and by realizing with joy the breadth and depth of what we might well be capable of.

This is what I'm calling Real Life. Real Life is about what happens when we fully engage with our everyday lives, whatever shape our lives take, whatever challenges and obstacles that life may bring.

Psychologist Carol Dweck, in her book *Mindset: The New Psychology of Success*, talks about a *mindset* as a set of beliefs that shapes how we make sense of the world and ourselves. These beliefs influence how we think, how we feel, and how we behave.

She describes a *fixed mindset* in this way:

> In a fixed mindset, people believe their basic qualities, like their intelligence or talent, are simply fixed traits. They spend their time documenting their intelligence or talent instead of developing them ... I've seen so many people with this one consuming goal of proving themselves—in the classroom, in their careers, and in their relationships. Every situation calls for a confirmation of their intelligence, personality, or character. Every situation is evaluated: Will I succeed or fail? Will I look smart or dumb? Will I be accepted or rejected? Will I feel like a winner or a loser?

She describes the *growth mindset* as this:

> There's another mindset in which these traits are not simply a hand you're dealt and have to live with, always trying to convince yourself and others that you have a royal flush when you're secretly worried it's a pair of tens. In this mindset, the hand you're dealt is just the starting point for development. This growth mindset is based on the belief that your basic qualities are things you can cultivate through your efforts.

In other words, if we want our lives to look different from the way they do, be more fulfilling, more authentic, less fixed and restricted, we have to believe in movement, in change, and in the possibility of development. If we think these serve no purpose, we're simply stuck.

✳

The Passover Seder, seen symbolically, provides a powerful metaphor for the journey to real life. It begins in the recognition of suffering and oppression, but instead of being defined by it, we engage it, and together, we find inspiration, and ultimately, aspiration for a better world. It's a ritual we repeat to renew our energy to go forward into life, rather than shrink away. We journey from confinement to freedom, from humiliation to dignity.

At the same time, the narrative framework I'm most familiar with for examining life's suffering and our chance for relief from suffering comes from the Buddha's teaching. Because it doesn't require adherence to a belief system, doesn't ask for loyalty, celebrates questioning, and invites one's own direct experience, I've always considered it more a psychological system than anything else. I refer to this framework a lot in this book because, for my entire adult life, I have found the perspective of Buddhist psychology immensely helpful in my effort to disentangle from painful habits, journey into the unknown with greater well-being, and nurture happiness and an experience of community. It has helped me have a sense of doing my best to live my life every day according to my deepest values.

An earlier book I wrote, *Real Love,* was about just that, love. *Real Change* was about systemic change, with an emphasis on linking inner change to change in the world. *Real Life* is about the inner journey—and journeys—we make when we decide to fully live life, whatever the world has presented to us, knowing that life is short and also that life is sacred.

We explore the journey to expansive freedom through working

with tools like mindful awareness, friendship, and the fostering of a greater sense of meaning in everyday life. These manifest in our lives as taking risks with what we dare to imagine, taking an interest in internal states we normally try to avoid, and taking an interest in people we normally try to avoid—as well as appreciation, accountability, and redefining community.

From a distance, or with a merely superficial look, a journey like this can seem just too formidable, with lots of pressure and impossible standards to live up to. Up close, actually pursuing it, making it real, it is a fantastic adventure. Most beautifully, it is an adventure that we get to have together.

1

FROM CONSTRICTION
TO EXPANSION

✳

W HEN I WAS NINE, my mother died, so during a chunk of my chaotic childhood, I lived with my paternal grandparents—immigrants from Poland, observant Jews. Most of the practices of the household, like not turning on the lights on Saturday, the Sabbath, I simply followed with little interest or curiosity about any possible deeper meaning. Following along suited my general sense of numbness anyway. The Passover Seder, however, was a big exception.

I didn't have a tremendous understanding of the layers of the Seder's symbolism or values—but I *felt* a lot. I felt a stirring of joy at the coming together of family (even if my family didn't look like the conventional picture I had in my head from TV), the tribal recognition of collective suffering (which painted a picture of a life I could actually feel I belonged within), the idea that life could be different, could be better, and that no matter how hard things were, you could imagine you were on your way to that better life.

I'd like to consider the Seder apart from religious identity, apart from leaning into the geopolitical realities of Israel, the Palestinian people, or Egyptians. I didn't know any of that as a frightened child, and even as an adult, if I am marking the Passover Seder in some way, it's my own way, with a consideration of all beings everywhere who are suffering, who seek a better life. The liturgical text, the Haggadah, that I've used for years is a Jewish Buddhist Haggadah, where quotations from Padmasambhava, who brought Buddhism from India to Tibet, and from the Buddha himself are laced throughout the depictions of the essential journey from bondage to liberation.

In Hebrew, the word conventionally translated as Egypt in the Haggadah is called *mitzrayim*. The name is derived from *m'tzarim*, meaning "narrow straits" (*mi*, "from"; *tzar*, "narrow" or "tight"): a place of constriction, tightness, limitation, or narrow-mindedness. Each of us lives, at least at times, in our own *mitzrayim*, the narrow straits of seeing few options, or being defined by someone else who has more power than we do in a situation, or feeling so unseen that we absorb someone's projection so thoroughly we come perilously close to forgetting who we are.

Perhaps we've been engulfed by a personal tragedy or health crisis, so that taking that first tentative step out of overwhelm toward an uncertain but beckoning future seems untenable. Or our actions are so determined by what we have been taught to believe in contrast to what we can newly discover that our ability to know wonder or awe seems completely beside the point.

Our personal Exodus is journeying out from an opaque world—where it's difficult to breathe, where change, the ever-present rhythm of life, is all too muffled, where the tight bindings around our hearts keep them from generously nourishing our bodies, our feelings, our entire existence—to a wholly different kind of world.

We journey from fixity to freedom.

CONTRACTION

CONTRACTION OR constriction isn't the same as focusing, being one-pointed, being centered, or being contained. We can be specific, determined, intentional, without being constricted.

Think of the last time you were lost in fear. The last time you were harshly unforgiving of yourself. The last time you felt trapped. The last time a craving was so strong that all reason and common sense fled (remember, for example, those old infatuations). The last time any sense of potential change collapsed and you fell into hopelessness. Those are times we experience limited options, the blunting of our creativity, a feeling of disconnection, the dimming of our vision of what is possible.

Judson Brewer, author of *Unwinding Anxiety*, once said to me, "My personal practice comes together with my lab's research in exploring the experience of contraction versus expansion and how that manifests in the world in so many ways."

Jud—who is a psychiatrist, neuroscientist, and director of research and innovation at the Mindfulness Center at Brown University—began by telling me about a dynamic web of interconnection in the brain called the *default mode network*. The posterior cingulate cortex (PCC)—the hub of self-referential habits—is a key part of this network. In his research, he found that "when people were feeling guilty, they activated the PCC. When they were craving a bunch of different substances, they activated it. When they were ruminating, they activated it. When they were anxious, they activated it."

What Jud and his team found was that the PCC correlated with a feeling of contraction: "The experience of anxiety, of guilt, of craving, of rumination—all of these—share literally an experiential component of contraction. We contract, and we close down."

None of this is to say that contraction is bad or wrong to feel. But if it becomes chronic, we begin living more and more in a world of tunnel vision, of auditory exclusion, of distorted perception, of narrowed interests, of joy that is right here in front of us that we miss simply because we don't see it. Our perception of options, of possibility, of aliveness, fades.

We suffer.

Learning to be aware of these narrow straits and changing how we respond to them is crucial. "If we read the news and read something that pisses us off, it is that reaction of contraction that feels bad," Jud explained. "So we may have this urge to make ourselves feel better by firing off a tweet, writing an email, eating a cupcake. This perpetuates the entire process. If we're not aware of our habitual responses, we not only may make things worse for ourselves, but also for society."

What we are working to evolve is an inner environment where we can surround that state of constriction, of holding back from the flow of life, with spaciousness, ease of heart, and kindness. Cultivating that radically changed relationship is the essence of the journey to being free.

ASSUMPTIONS

THE QUALITY of our lives can be limited by the thought patterns that produce much of our constriction, such as unexamined assumptions. Sometimes—perhaps most of the time—we don't even notice the ideas we hold about ourselves, our experiences, our friends, family, and so on. We tend to accept our preconceptions, judgments, hasty conclusions, and anxieties about the world as truth: ultimate, unyielding, inflexible. Our world shrinks, becoming ever smaller and smaller.

※

My friend Friedrike Merck is a sculptor. One year, she told me that she had a piece in the National Gallery of Art in Washington, D.C., so on a visit to the capital, I went to see it. I walked up and down and up and down the vast corridors of the museum. I checked every room, looked at each display case and pedestal— and I just couldn't find it! My mind went everywhere, all the way to, *Just my luck. I have to be the one to break the news to her that they decided not to put it up after all. It must be in a basement somewhere.* Having given up in disappointment, as I headed for the exit, I casually glanced up at a wall—and there was her beautiful piece. It was a bas-relief, not the freestanding piece I'd expected: my assumptions had contoured my vision, and determined what I was expecting to see, and what I was simply *not* seeing.

Several of the traditions found in India use a well-known parable: Someone walks along a path. They casually look ahead and see a poisonous snake barring their way and turn and run in the opposite direction. As they return along the same path in the morning, they see that same shape but look more carefully and find a coiled rope on the ground. There never was a snake. Or as *Star Wars* Jedi knight Obi-Wan Kenobi said, "Your eyes can deceive you . . ."

Because of many factors, including previous traumatic experience, we might be easily activated by the ropes littered throughout our lives, mistaking each for a source of the highest danger. When that's the case, we rarely feel safe. It's exhausting, so the times when we really do see a snake and mistake it for a harmless piece of rope (which actually happened to me once in Burma, only for me to be saved by a group of Burmese women who shooed me away from an outdoor staircase where a highly poisonous green snake was taking a nap, masquerading as a piece of yarn), we might not be able to summon the acuity we need to protect ourselves.

One day not long ago, I was on a Zoom call with friends and (perhaps inelegantly) drinking seltzer straight from a can. At one point, one of my friends said, "Why are you drinking beer at 10:00 a.m.?" I held up the can next to the camera and protested, "It's not beer; it's seltzer." Afterward, I reflected how glad I was that she'd asked. In another context, not with friends, I might have started sensing innuendoes in snatches of conversations, fielding offers of help, and been puzzled about why people started acting strangely around me.

Questioning our assumptions doesn't leave us full of doubt and uncertainty, floundering, unable to take a step in any direction. It leaves us in a more spacious place, released from the grip of perhaps having once, long ago, felt a certain way, or from projecting our fears into a seemingly unchanging future, or from making choices based on something like a long-ago determination that we don't deserve to be happy. Questioning leaves us free to examine, explore, and experiment.

What do you think the messages you've received are—about who you are, how you're designated, about where you belong, who you're capable of becoming?

Zainab Salbi—an Iraqi American women's rights activist, humanitarian, author, founder of Women for Women International, and co-founder of Daughters for Earth—articulates beautifully the limitations of relying on the external assumptions we so easily grasp at, and what it meant for her to break free of that. Zainab had been building Women for Women International since her early twenties. By the time she reached her forties, it had grown from a small operation (with her husband and a handful of volunteers working out of her in-laws' basement) into an award-winning humanitarian organization with seven hundred staff and offices in ten countries, helping hundreds of thousands of women survivors of wars and distributing millions of dollars in aid.

However, even with all she had achieved, she writes in her book *Freedom Is an Inside Job: Owning Our Darkness and Our Light to Heal Ourselves and the World*, "Inside I felt like a failure." In particular, she was deeply dismayed by the fact that would-be donors "seemed to prefer seeing their destitution, torn clothes, devastated faces, blood and dirt. Pity raised money . . . but it did not get women's voices heard, dignity seen, or strength witnessed."

She became ashamed of her feelings of frustration and failure and did not want to admit them to anyone, even her therapist. Her mind raced. She was restless, and "perhaps to avoid a deeper encounter with my own heart," she booked herself with more and more work and social activity, until she reached the point where "even distracting myself became irritating. It was time to explore my feelings further. To do that, I needed the safety of silence."

Even though she knew nothing about Zen meditation, she booked herself into a four-day retreat. She felt that a stately house in the woods would provide a safe place for her to ruminate. On the first day, she writes:

I experienced a torrent of painful feelings, all of which I wanted to avoid. I had meditated at home before, following tips from friends or yoga classes or videos I had seen online, but just for ten minutes at a time. As I sat for hours on the small, round cushions on the floor that first day, every part of my body ached. My mind rebelled. I fixated on other participants' every movement to try to distract myself from going inward. When someone sighed or sneezed or shifted their body, I noticed. It was easier to pay attention to the details of the pattern in the carpet or the sound of the copper bell that marked the time than to ask myself the questions I came to ask.

Over the course of the four days, though, the silence began to take over, and she began to see her shame in a clearer light:

It was the shame of missing my mark, of doing more talking than accomplishing; the shame of not being as successful as my successful friends; the worry that people might feel bad for me or look down on me or that I might have to give up on my big dreams and just be content with what I had accomplished so far.

By day two, seeing all the thoughts from every angle was illuminating but also "like going through a storage room full of clutter." She investigated the arising thoughts in a fresh way in the silent space: "If worry came, I checked out why I was worried. What was the story behind the worry? Where did it come from? Was it real or not real? I stayed with the feeling until I had processed and digested it, and then I let it go."

Gradually, she worked through her restlessness and "desire to accomplish more than I was currently able to do." What emerged from the retreat was insight about what really held her in its grip:

> Our attachments to whom we think we're supposed to be are like chains around our necks. Our identities get wrapped up in the external roles, titles, and accomplishments that we put value on . . . A wealthy businessman values how much he's worth financially. A research scientist values the cure she is working on. A writer values the books he writes and publishes. In my case, I valued how much social change I could create through my advocacy for women's rights and my humanitarian work.
>
> At first, it might seem that one pursuit or identity is more valuable than another. Surely, the cure for a disease is more important than how many books an author sells. Surely, creating social change that improves thousands—if not millions—of lives is more important than increasing the wealth of one individual. At a fundamental level, though, no matter what our vocation is, our accomplishments are where we find our core self-value and feel affirmed.
>
> Attachments are attachments, I realized, no matter who we are or what we identify with. When we value ourselves because of what we accomplish and how much we accomplish, our souls are forever held hostage to these attachments. No matter how much we do, how many dollars we accumulate, cures we discover, books we sell, or people we help, it is never going to be enough to permanently fulfill us. . . .
>
> I was completely identified with my work, and in my own mind, I could never be successful enough at it. That was a very big chain around my soul, a huge weight on my

being. Realizing this was like cutting the umbilical cord to my shame. . . .

One short silent retreat couldn't instantly change the shape of my life—or my mind. It had just given me a taste of what freedom from attachments could be like. It was like tasting chocolate for the first time: we can't describe how good it tastes until we've actually tasted it, and then we can't ever forget that taste. Now that I had seen the source of my pain and the route to my freedom, I had a clear path to follow.

As Zainab's story so powerfully illustrates, we can learn to recognize assumptions for the thoughts that they are, rather than cleaving to them as an ultimate defining reality we're bound to. We get to choose, "Do I want to take this to heart or let it go?"

EXPANSION

ONE TIME when my colleague Joseph Goldstein and I were visiting a friend in Houston, we all went out to a restaurant to order takeout. As we were waiting for the food to be prepared, Joseph struck up a conversation with the young man working behind the counter. After a few minutes, he told Joseph that he'd never left Houston and went on to describe, somewhat passionately, how his dream was to one day go to Wyoming. When Joseph asked him what he thought he would find there, he responded, "Open, expansive space, a feeling of being unconfined, with peacefulness and freedom and room to move."

Joseph responded, "There's an inner Wyoming, too, you know."

At that point, the young man fixed a stare at Joseph and said, "That's freaky," as he sidled away.

But there *is* an inner Wyoming, a potential for openness, spaciousness, clarity, and freedom that exists within each of us. We just need confidence in it, to make the journey to that place, to discover it, nurture it, and hold the memory that it's there, waiting for us to visit anytime.

In moving from contraction to spaciousness, it's as if we're sitting in a narrow, low-ceilinged, dark room—so accustomed to it that we don't even realize we're confined—and then the door swings open, revealing light, room to move, and possibilities that suddenly await. We don't know just what is out there, but it's certainly more vast and spacious than that tiny room.

My favorite way of imagining that expansive state—as someone with asthma—is "being able to breathe again." More than just pleasure, different from indulgence, it is mostly a sensation of huge relief. It is peace.

Theologian Howard Thurman recommended that we "look at the world with quiet eyes." It's an intriguing phrase. It seems like with the way we so often look at the world, we resemble cartoon characters whose eyes are popping out on springs: "I see something I want! Give it to me!" Our heads rapidly turn to the object of our desire in a fixed gaze, so as not to lose sight of it. Our bodies lean forward in anticipation. Our arms extend, reaching out to acquire it. Our fingers flex, ready to grab on to what we want, to try to keep it from changing, from eluding our grasp. Our shoulders strain to hold on even tighter.

That's grasping, contraction.

It happens in a moment, or an hour, or a day, a month, a lifetime—and it brings a lot of pain.

So, look at the world with quiet eyes whenever you can, and let go of grasping. The world will come to fill you without your straining for it. In that relaxation, you will find peace. Peace isn't a fabricated state, repressing all woes and challenges. It is tuning into our fundamental nature.

Willa Maile Qimeng Cuthrell-Tuttleman, when she was seven years old and a student at Friends Academy in Manhattan, wrote a poem that beautifully expresses what I understand as peace.

Peace Is Friendship

    Peace looks like nature
    Peace smells like fresh air
    Peace sounds like wind blowing through the trees
    Peace tastes like bubble gum
    Peace feels like a soft pillow

I have a friend who describes himself as pretty obsessive when nursing a grudge, another contracted state. He can go over and over and over the words of the misunderstanding, or his resentment at not being included, or someone's reckless behavior. Over and over and over. After one such interlude, he reflected on the obsessive quality, declaring:

"I let him live rent-free in my brain for too long."

Now imagine yourself going home to that blessedly quiet apartment of your mind. What a relief. You can play music. You can cuddle with your dog. You can reach out to a struggling friend. You can cook a meal, or write a poem, or maybe finally get some sleep.

Expansiveness doesn't lead us to a vacuous place—cavernous, muted, disconnected. Expansiveness isn't being spaced out, floating above it all. In the sense that I'm using the word, expansiveness is energized, confident, creative, brimming with love. The subtle balances in life—of rest and action, of passion and letting go, of the power of intention and of patience—all can take place in this expansive space.

Expansiveness helps broaden our perspective, so we can think more flexibly and with a more open mind. We become better able to focus on the big picture and not feel so discouraged by the constant array of ups and downs we experience every day. When faced with adversity, we can generate more solutions. Expansiveness invites experimentation and imagination. We're more willing to pour ourselves fully into life's pursuits. It is the freedom of letting down the burden we have been carrying. It leaves room for our fundamentally loving hearts to uncoil, and lead us onward.

✳

Reflecting on the contrast between contraction and expansion, a friend of mine, Linda Stone, whom we will learn more about in chapter 6, related it to the difference between knowledge and feeling. She said:

> I've put so much focus on accumulating knowledge in my life . . . and, sometimes, when it comes through playful curiosity, it can be expansive. But so much more often, it's been reductionist, mentally centered, and it can be contracting, and actually block feeling. Holding on to bits of knowledge sometimes seems like the enemy of possibility. Direct experience/feeling seems more expansive. I've also been thinking about how the habit of accomplishing and accumulating relates to self-worth. In part because of the COVID lockdown, I stepped back into more of a "retired" state than I have ever been in: more being, less doing. That's been accompanied by the need to reformulate the externally based calculations of worth: credentials, goals,

affiliations. The mind can be a badgering, contracting bully. And no amount of "knowledge," as I've tried to amass it, ever seems to really shift this. Moment-to-moment presence—which usually offers wonder, awe, appreciation—feels like an expansive antidote.

When the astronaut Mae Jemison talks about literal "space," I hear a beautiful evocation of expansiveness: "Once I got into space, I was feeling very comfortable in the universe. I felt like I had the right to be anywhere in this universe, that I belonged here as much as any speck of stardust, any comet, any planet."

※

Many years ago, I attended a stress-reduction program led by Jon Kabat-Zinn, longtime meditation teacher and founder of Mindfulness-Based Stress Reduction. In one exercise, he stepped up to the blackboard, and in the center, he drew a square made up of nine dots, arranged in three parallel lines with three dots in each line. He then challenged everyone in the class to take the piece of chalk and see if we could connect all the dots using only four straight lines, without removing the chalk from the blackboard, and without retracing a line. One by one, all thirty of us went up to the blackboard. We tried beginning from the left, from the right, from the top, from the bottom, and returned to our seats frustrated, unable to do what he'd asked. The room was vibrating with stress.

Then Jon picked up the chalk and, with great sweeping strokes that extended well beyond the perimeter of the small square, did exactly what he had challenged us to do. Every one of us had presumed that to succeed we had to stay within the circumscribed area formed by the nine dots. Jon had never said that we were limited to that little space, but all of us had concluded that was the only area we could move within, the only place to find options. Not one of us could see beyond our limited sense of how much room we had to work in.

HOW MUCH ROOM DO WE HAVE?

WHEN THE Buddha taught 2,600 years ago, the social structure in India was built on a rigid philosophical system. According to their prevailing view of the world, everything and every being belonged to a predetermined category or class, and each of these had its own essential nature and its corresponding duty in life or role to play. For example, it is the nature of fire to be hot and to warm and burn things, of rocks to be hard and to support, of grass to grow and provide sustenance to animals, of cows to eat grass and produce milk. The responsibility of every being was to grow into its own nature and to conform to an ideal disposition specific to them. These natures and duties were considered immutable truths. That's one meaning of the word *dharma:* that predetermined, preordained nature.

Socially, this concept was translated into the rigidities of the caste system. People were born destined to fulfill a certain nature. It was the duty of certain classes or castes of people to rule, for Brahmans to mediate with divine forces, and for certain other people to be engaged in producing food and material goods. Within this worldview, actions conceived of as moral and appropriate for one caste or gender were considered completely immoral for another. It was proper and beneficial for the Brahman male to read and study the scriptures, while this was absolutely forbidden and considered abhorrent for someone in the "untouchable" caste, an outcast.

Into this constricting social context, the Buddha introduced his revolutionary teachings. What he taught in terms of ethics was radical then, and it is radical now. He asserted that what determines whether an action is moral or immoral is the volition of the person performing it. The moral quality of an action is held within the intention that gives rise to the action. "Not by birth is one a Brahman, or an outcast," the Buddha said, "but by deeds." This teaching, in effect, declared the entire social structure of India, considered sacrosanct by many, to be of no spiritual significance at all.

The Buddha was declaring that the only status that truly matters is the status of personal goodness, and personal goodness is attained through personal effort, not by birth. It did not matter if you were a man or a woman, wealthy or poor, a Brahman or an outcast—an action based on greed would have a certain kind of result, and an action based on love would have a certain kind of result. "A true Brahman is one who is gentle, who is wise and caring," he said, thus completely negating the importance of caste, skin color, class, and gender in any consideration of morality.

It is fascinating and poignant to see how much each of these elements can be a factor in assessing our own or someone else's worth today, all these years later and throughout the world. In this one teaching, the Buddha burst the bubble of social class, of deflecting responsibility, of mindless deference to religious authority, and of defining potential according to external criteria. In this one teaching, he returned the potential for freedom back to each one of us.

WE HAVE A LOT OF ROOM

THAT'S ANOTHER meaning of the word *dharma:* actualizing that potential for freedom we all have, shedding the stories others have told about us to discover who we genuinely are, understanding what we care about most deeply, what makes for a better life. Dharma is not something we are fated to, or stoic about, but the very set of practices that can lift us out of our conditioning, out of an assumed set of limits and away from what is often a pervasive resignation. We can see for ourselves the elements of life that sustain us, bring us closer and closer to the truth of how things are. Rather than the fixed assignment we are given at birth, dharma reflects a breathtaking capacity of any one of us to take a journey away from constriction and resignation to a vital, creative, free life. None of this is determined in the external conditions of who we are; it is all held in the universal potential of who we might become.

To breathe life into dharma in this sense is the journey of liberation we make. Step by step, we move toward freedom and we manifest freedom all at the same time.

THERE ARE MANY MODELS OF JOURNEYING TO LIVE A FULL AND FREE LIFE, A REAL LIFE . . .

SOME ARE faith-based; others are completely secular. They all provide a vision of a life that is not just lived mechanically, driven by habit—unfulfilled or disconnected. They all say, in effect, that we don't have to be so perpetually lonely, feel so boxed in, so circumscribed. In one way or another, these depictions of a journey to freedom evoke an ability to look at one's circumstances and not be bound by them, to begin to imagine a life other than the one dictated to us by the world. I've often said that I think we live in a time of commonly blunted aspiration, where we don't dare dream of much, but here greater aspiration awakens. We don't just *receive* the story of our lives, we *discover* a new sense of agency in the writing or rewriting of it—a telling that reflects both the universality of that story and its own unique distinctiveness. Psychologist Abraham Maslow said, "It would seem that every human being comes at birth into society not as a lump of clay to be molded by society, but rather as a structure which society may warp or suppress or build upon. We're here to make a rose into a good rose, not turn a rose into a lily."

So how do we live more fully as ourselves, with growing purpose and interest and joy? While Maslow's work is well known and has been widely shared, I find it helpful to revisit his model of growth viewed through a progressive fulfilling of a hierarchy of needs, as we consider contraction and expansion:

1. *Physiological*—These are biological requirements for human survival, such as air, food, drink, shelter, clothing, warmth, sleep.

2. *Safety*—Emotional security, financial security (for example, employment, social welfare), freedom from fear, social stability, health and well-being. The need for safety is the basis of all other needs. Safety means stability, a sense of having trust in our environment. This secure foundation allows us to take risks and go out and explore the world.

3. *Love and belonging*—Examples of belonging needs include friendship, intimacy, trust, acceptance, receiving and giving affection, and love. Feeling connection to others is a fundamental need. The quality of connection hinges on what psychologist Carl Rogers refers to as "unconditional positive regard," which occurs when a person feels seen, cared for, and safe expressing a whole range of feelings and experiences.

4. *Esteem*—Includes self-worth, accomplishment, and respect. This includes first esteem for oneself (dignity, achievement, mastery, independence) and, second, the desire for reputation or respect from others (status and prestige, for example). It comes down to liking yourself!

5. *Self-actualization*—Refers to the realization of a person's potential for self-fulfillment, bringing personal growth and peak experiences, referring to experiences that bring an increase in wonder, joy, serenity, and a heightened sense of beauty while also creating a deeper connection with the world around us. We have these potentialities within us that we can feel deep inside and that could offer so much benefit to ourselves and to the world. Self-actualization is living with openness and curiosity, bringing those potential realities to as full expression as possible.

To journey well, instead of being driven by perpetual discontent, anxieties, and battling with reality because of a sense of deficiency, we are increasingly accepting and loving of ourselves and others. The journey becomes more about *What choices will lead me to greater integration and wholeness?* than about anything else.

NO JOURNEY IS EXCLUSIVELY LINEAR

IN SPEAKING about the hierarchy of needs later in his life, Maslow emphasized that order in the hierarchy "is not nearly as rigid" as he may have implied in his earlier work, that we needn't first completely fulfill one level of need to move on to the next.

Cognitive psychologist Scott Barry Kaufman, whom we will meet again in chapter 5, took a new look at Maslow's hierarchy of needs in his book *Transcend* and made this point: "He was very clear that human development is a constant developmental process where we move two steps forward, and then we fall back a step. Life is not like a video game where you reach one level like connection and then some voice from above is like, *Congrats, you've unlocked esteem and then we never have to worry about that again.* He's very clear life is not like that."

✳

The Buddhist journey to freedom is described in what is called the Eightfold Path, covering our everyday behavior, our mindfulness, and how we see the world. (See appendix on page 175.) My colleague Sylvia Boorstein—who has been teaching meditation for many decades and has written several books, including *Pay Attention, for Goodness' Sake: Practicing the Perfections of the Heart*—once referred to the Eightfold Path as "the Eightfold Dot," to help us move away from being stuck in a highly linear sense of a path: "Oh, I did those first few steps a while ago. They are elementary. I've moved on, way beyond those now."

Instead, Sylvia was pointing to cycles, to returning, to renewal and venturing deeper each time we are back once again. I find that a useful reminder whenever I commit to a journey, or a project, or an endeavor, so that I can loosen the grip of inherited models of "success" and "failure."

Instead of a linear model that evokes moving determinedly in just one direction, I've started to imagine the shape of the path to liberation as akin to a double helix, with strands that wrap around each other almost as a kind of twisted ladder. It's a path that is more integrated and circular, with elements crossing over at multiple points, reciprocally and mutually.

In Southeast Asia, there is a common story about someone

who goes into the forest to try to capture a bird. As the parable unfolds, the attempted capture is unsuccessful, *but it's not fruitless.* It turns out that it's fine if the person doesn't actually capture the bird. The lesson is that because of all the wandering through the forest, the seeker of the bird has learned the ways of the forest. Just so, if we wander as consciously as we can, whether we "succeed" or "fail," every moment counts. I've wanted to learn the ways of a meaningful life since I was eighteen years old. It hasn't been a straight line, and yet I haven't wavered about whether it was worth it.

PROVISIONS FOR THE JOURNEY

AS RABBI Nachman of Breslov, the famous Ukrainian religious leader from the late eighteenth and early nineteenth century, counseled, when you are about to leave *mitzrayim,* you should not worry about how you will manage in a new "place." Anyone who does or who stops to get everything in order prior to embarking on the journey will never pick himself or herself up.

A few years ago, I sat at the bedside of a friend a couple of weeks before she died. She was at home, and her hospital bed had been set up in the dining room. The door was open onto the garden, letting in a gentle breeze and the sound of birdsong as her life ebbed away. She was floating in and out of consciousness, and after a period of silence, she turned to me somewhat distraught and said, "I have to move all my things across the street."

"What do you mean?" I asked.

"It's complicated!" she replied.

I didn't know what she was talking about and didn't know what to say. I told her how much people loved her, how much I loved her. An hour passed, and it finally struck me what "across the street" probably meant. At that point, I said, "Remember when you told me you had to move all your things across the street and that it was complicated? Actually, you don't have to move all your things. You can go across the street without them. It will be okay."

"Really?" she asked.

"I'm sure," I told her.

She died peacefully not so long after. I've thought about her comment many times since, in a variety of circumstances, as an inspiration to help me let go.

Our tendency to cling to the stuff of this world pushes us to drag our things—physical possessions, emotional baggage, old assumptions, and habitual reactions—through every transition. It is hard to contemplate letting go, let alone letting go of absolutely everything, as we cross the street of mortality. No wonder we think of change as the enemy!

Letting go—even of what we don't need—in order to journey on can be an intricate process. If we harshly demand it of ourselves, it can easily morph into feigned disinterest, or withdrawal and the refusal to feel. But letting go is not about refusing to feel, or not caring, or turning away from those we love. It is not about disconnecting or disassociating from our own experience, whatever that looks like. Letting go is profoundly honest, grounded firmly in the truth of what is. That's why it is such a release. By the time we reach this stage, we are beyond the need or desire for an agenda. We have no time or use for manipulating.

SATURDAY NIGHT SEDER

IN THE spring of 2020, with COVID raging (and my having asthma), I pretty much just sheltered in place in Barre, Massachusetts, seeing very few (and only masked) people, sitting at a distance. As Passover approached, it was clear I wasn't going to be gathering with anyone. Amazingly, there was a show on YouTube called *Saturday Night Seder*, created as a benefit for the CDC Foundation, a non-profit that supports the work of the Centers for Disease Control and Prevention. It was an incredible time to be watching the story of a journey taken by people with very few options from confinement to expansive liberation!

It was one of the very early productions to make use of a Zoom writing room, with people recording offerings on personal smartphones and tablets. I loved it. It featured world-class singers; amusing sidenotes to the ritual (as if you were in a home with friends); rabbis reminding us of the primary question "What can you do for people who are suffering, since you once suffered?"; historical references (people looking at the era when "Over the Rainbow" was composed have suggested parallels between the lyrics and the experience of Jews during Kristallnacht and the rise of Nazism). It brought me to laughter and to tears.

And it instilled in me a conviction that this journey—from confinement to freedom, from constraint to openness, from isolation to community—is our fundamental, essential journey, the one that we bring to life over and over again. To once again quote Rabbi Nachman:

The Exodus from Egypt occurs in every human being, in every era, in every year, and in every day.

2

WHEN DO WE FEEL
THE SMALLEST?

✳

I T'S OFTEN HARD to be a human being and to figure out how
to do it well. That's true for our impatient neighbor, our narcis-
sistic boss, our delightful friend, the street musicians we see playing
on our way to the bus, the bus driver, and all those we encounter
along the way.

And it is also true for ourselves.

Consciously or unconsciously, we yearn for something beyond the flashing elation of success, the calculated measure of

accumulation, the intermittent delight of sensual satisfaction. All of these might be great, even as they are ephemeral, but we can have a whole lot more: a power of happiness that is a wellspring within, affording us a sense of belonging, wholeness, and peace.

As human beings, living day to day, we all could have more than fleeting pleasure or compromised joy, and something more truly fulfilling than the bitter taste of seeking control and then watching control wrested away from us by inevitable change.

It's not necessarily the yearning itself that is problematic for us. Rather, we struggle and feel lost and discontented because we don't know exactly where our greatest happiness can be found, because we're often being taught to aim so badly in search of fulfillment. We needn't feel squeamish or ashamed of our longing for a greater, more profound happiness. We don't have to see it as weak, or diminishing, or something that will hold us back. In fact, we need to take hold of that longing, expand it through greater understanding, and empower it to help us be brave in seeking a good life. As Mother Teresa said, "Don't give up the right to be happy. Don't ever give it up."

There are moments when we sense the glimmering of a different tomorrow beckoning or acutely feel the constraint of anxiety we've been holding for what seems like forever, and we think, *I'm going to make a move.* We might begin to believe the self-talk that has been saying, *You can't do this . . . and oh, by the way . . . you can't do that either,* can shift, or that the sadness we've been carrying doesn't need to define us anymore. There are times when we feel— with sudden conviction—that we could become a lot happier than we have been, more at peace, less afraid.

The journey we make is propelled throughout by these shifts in our worldview—our sense of who we are, what's important in life, how alone we are, where strength is to be found, where happiness is to be found. Sometimes that shift is big and fast;

sometimes it seems awfully small. In either case, it can be enough to spur movement.

That shift is an acknowledgment of possibility that allows us to engage without a promise of definite, immediate reward. It is an opening. This is what gets us out of bed, away from inertia, to see if life can be a little bit different—or even a lot different. This is the dynamism that reminds us to imagine what might yet be rather than allowing despair, discouragement, or sullen withdrawal to lay waste to any sense of possibility.

In commenting on the journey of Aeneas, the hero of Virgil's epic poem about the founding of Rome, the late Irish poet and priest John O'Donohue talks about Aeneas setting out while not yet knowing where he was going. Only when he has the courage to step into the darkness, as O'Donohue poetically depicts it, does the light to guide the next step reveal itself. Though we might repeatedly stumble, afraid to move forward into the unknown, into uncertainty, we can do it for one step, and then another, if our view of what's fixed and what is malleable can keep adjusting.

We take that step in the darkness because of an inkling, perhaps faint, uncertain, but alive. We feel inspired. Or perhaps we simply feel tired of being confined.

Being in the narrow place I described in the first chapter does not refer to being one-pointed, purposeful, determined, or focused. By a "narrow place," I want to convey the feeling of being trapped. In Buddhist psychology, the three main hindrances to a life of freedom are described as grasping, aversion, and delusion. They're called *hindrances* because if we're immersed in them, they hinder our ability to live fully, to spend a day in appreciation of what is, to respond to circumstances with resonance and depth. In their thrall, we chase shadows, trying to find abiding happiness. We see ourselves only as we imagine others see us. We helplessly repeat patterns despite their leaving us feeling sidelined rather than in the dynamic center of life.

When we're entangled in one or more of these three states—not simply when we feel them, not even when we feel them intensely, but when we become overcome or defined by them—the natural consequence is a state of fixation, of tunnel vision, of overlooking many real chances for happiness while being beguiled by beliefs or behaviors that don't deliver much.

THE WRONG PLACES AND
THE WRONG WAYS

ONCE, I WAS traveling back to the East Coast from New Mexico with some friends and their four-year-old child when she unaccountably wandered off in the St. Louis airport and got lost. We were all frantically running around looking for her. Finally, over the loudspeaker came the announcement: "Would you please come find your daughter at Gate 2." When we got there, we found the child extremely upset and frightened. She said accusingly to her mother, "You weren't where you were supposed to be."

In fact, her mother had never left where she was supposed to be, and the child herself had wandered off. The incident reminded me of the sense of betrayal and fear we can feel when we discover that perfect happiness isn't where we had expected it to be: *You're not where you are supposed to be!*

Ironically, it is sometimes society's precise prescriptions for freedom, for happiness, and for abundance that bind us most severely. It is in part because we need to face down the myths and distortions taught to us that we call it a journey.

In some way, these three root hindrances are like qualities of misplaced faith or misplaced trust. It's as though when we're lost within any of these three states, we offer our hearts to the wrong things or in the wrong ways.

In craving or grasping, we place our hearts upon an object or an experience in the fervent belief that it will satisfy us forever, providing the lasting satisfaction we long for. That's what we place our faith on.

In aversion (anger and fear), we place our hearts upon the ability to separate ourselves from what is happening, to somehow declare it untrue or declare it apart from us. We place our faith on the ability to have control over things, to keep unpleasant experiences from happening, to be able to cut them off.

In delusion, we place our hearts upon not noticing, on not seeing the truth of things. We feel protected by not seeing impermanence, not seeing how one thing leads to the next. We place our trust or our faith in not feeling much of anything and somehow muddling through.

Another way to see these states when they've become habitual patterns—quickly arising in times of stress or difficulty, swiftly defining and limiting our options for responding—is as adaptations. If we're beginning to encounter some real pain and don't have the confidence that we can make our way through, one way or another, we dance around it. We acquire something to distract ourselves with, in an attempt to avoid the pain in order to feel powerful or retreat into numbness. Some adaptations can be quite intelligent, and some herald survival (as we see in the many accounts of people abused as children who basically cease to fully inhabit their bodies). However, when these adaptations become our *sole* response, resorted to again and again, outliving their usefulness, they become that narrow strait, holding us in a confined place. As the late writer and activist Audre Lorde said, "Pain is important: how we evade it, how we succumb to it, how we deal with it, how we transcend it."

Many different habitual reactions can serve as mechanisms to help us delay or disregard the experience of pain: pulling back into disconnection; splaying the pain outward by casting blame; clinging to consumerism, overwork, risk-taking, substances, speediness. I remember a time when I was sitting with some war veterans and their families. There was a remarkable woman whose son had suffered a severe injury. She was talking so fast I could barely follow her, at a really frenetic pace, and her words seemed driven by a passionate intensity: "I saved my son's life, I told his doctors . . . I told his surgeons . . . He would have died without me. I got him out of the hospital, though. I got him out of that bed!" At warp speed. I kept thinking, *Wow, I wonder what would happen if she slowed down. There might then be a huge world of pain to encounter.*

We've all done something like this in one way or another in really difficult circumstances. Choosing to slow down in an instance like that is complex and delicate. And it absolutely needs to emerge from the person feeling the pain most directly. Slowing down cannot be forced on someone. We don't know their situation. We ourselves, though, sometimes want the option of not being so compelled to act in one particular way. We want to spread our wings, take a step or two into being different. We want to integrate *all* of our experience, however joyful or painful, and journey through life as a whole person. For that, we need to understand our strongest patterns.

GRASPING

GRASPING ENCOMPASSES:

- our conditioning to hold on tightly to something—an experience, an object, a person—as a futile totem against change;

- the feeling of never *having* enough;
- the feeling of never *being* enough; and
- falling into addictive patterns.

All too often, we cling to people, experiences, and objects as though we could glue them in place, while ignoring the precipice of change we're standing on.

I'm using the words *craving* and *grasping* synonymously, and want to distinguish them from intentionality, from desiring to do something, being wholehearted or passionate about accomplishing something. Strong intention is ethically neutral: it causes us suffering and constriction *or* it brings us closer to expansion and freedom, depending on what accompanies it—greed or love, fear or wisdom.

Craving, by contrast, is by its very nature constricting. It moves us to obsess about what we don't have and overlook what we do have, so that we feel little appreciation or gratitude. It also elicits clinging to a person or object or experience in an attempt to deny and defy the truth of change. Good luck with that! Grasping narrows our sense of where happiness is to be found. (*It must be exactly this or I won't be happy.*) It binds us to fixation and frustration.

> *Set the bird's wings with gold and it will*
> *never again soar in the sky.*
>
> —RABINDRANATH TAGORE

Addiction

According to Dr. Jud Brewer, the psychiatrist and neuroscientist we met in the last chapter:

The simple definition of addiction is this:

continued use despite adverse consequences.

Continued tweeting despite adverse consequences. Continued shopping despite adverse consequences. Continued pining away for that special someone despite adverse consequences. Continued computer gaming despite adverse consequences. Continued eating despite adverse consequences.

And of course, alcohol and drugs, a realm where many experience the adverse consequences in the form of genuine tragedy. It's an inexpressible sorrow that an effort to avoid suffering can result in so much breakage—of relationships, of dreams, of lives.

Of course, not everything we reach for to get some sleep or find a break from harrowing thoughts becomes an addiction. Which brings us back to craving. The texture and flavor of craving or grasping is captured well in the classical Tibetan image of "the Wheel of Life." It is a representation of many realms making up a bigger picture of life—those characterized chiefly by craving, by jealousy, by anger, by balance, or by delight. The slice of life heavily marked by craving is known as *the realm of hungry ghosts.*

The dwellers in that realm are pictured as wraiths with tiny little mouths, narrow necks, and enormous bellies. They are built to be insatiable. So much wanting all of the time, so little satisfaction. It's a brutal existence of relentless neediness.

Dr. Gabor Maté named his book on addiction *In the Realm of Hungry Ghosts,* and in it he writes:

Not all addictions are rooted in abuse or trauma, but I do believe they can all be traced to painful experience. A hurt is at the centre of all addictive behaviours. It is present in the gambler, the Internet addict, the compulsive shopper and the workaholic. The wound may not be as deep and the ache not as excruciating, and it may even be entirely hidden—but it's there.

At the core of every addiction is an emptiness based in abject fear. The addict dreads and abhors the present moment; she bends feverishly only toward the next time, the moment when her brain, infused with her drug of choice, will briefly experience itself as liberated from the burden of the past and the fear of the future—the two elements that make the present intolerable. Many of us resemble the drug addict in our ineffectual efforts to fill in the spiritual black hole, the void at the centre, where we have lost touch with our souls, our spirit—with those sources of meaning and value that are not contingent or fleeting ... Not every story has a happy ending ... but the discoveries of science, the teachings of the heart, and the revelations of the soul all assure us that no human being is ever beyond redemption. The possibility of renewal exists so long as life exists. How to support that possibility in others and in ourselves is the ultimate question.

Buried somewhere in the midst of craving, there is a love of life, an ability to abandon oneself into experience, no withholding, no dealmaking. If we can learn how to work with the craving, we can recapture that.

A foundational practice that can be useful in lots of circumstances is being able to center our attention on a few breaths in a row, even if we're right in the middle of a conversation or a meeting or a surge of craving. It helps us pause, let go of distractions, and get a little space from our thoughts and feelings so we can then decide which of them we want to pursue. You can consider exploring this in meditation practice to have greater familiarity and ease with it in more pressured or anxious situations. (For a foundational breath meditation, see the meditation guide in the appendix on page 176.)

✳

I want to offer as many tools as I can to work with confining, limiting states throughout this book, including this one about craving from clinical psychologist Sarah Bowen, part of the team responsible for developing Mindfulness-Based Relapse Prevention, whose principles are reflected in this practice.

REFLECTIVE PRACTICE: SURF THE URGE

For people with histories of addiction, when the craving comes, it can feel as though you've already failed. A lot of people think, *I shouldn't even want this anymore, and now I'm having these thoughts about it and my body's doing something and I'm scared because I want this thing and I shouldn't.*

The craving can feel threatening. The practice we call Urge Surfing is sitting with yourself and being with the experience, and realizing that you *can* tolerate it. It's not pleasant, but you can feel it and stay with it, and you don't have to react in the usual way. You actually do have a choice in how you respond. It's physiological, it's conditioning, and it's not your fault. It's going to happen. The real questions to ask:

I'm experiencing this, and how can I really help myself get through this?

What does it actually feel like?

What is so uncomfortable?

What is so scary about this?

What does that feel like in my body?

What is my mind doing?

Can I stay with that and notice it may pass? It may come back again, and it may pass again.

The craving urge often has a tinge of panic to it, an urgency that's acute, so there's a need that's very real. Part of this practice is being with the strong sense of reactivity or urge or craving and then also asking yourself:

What do I really need here?

There is a strong guiding need here. Maybe I don't actually need this *substance*, but there is a deeper need: I need to feel better, or I need safety, or I need some validation.

AVERSION

AVERSION ENCOMPASSES:

- free-floating anxiety;

- habitual resentment;

- a punishing attitude toward ourselves and others rather than looking for rehabilitation or healing; and

- a perpetual seeing of what's wrong, rather than also allowing what's right.

We can be aversive, impatient, and unkind to ourselves as well as others, or embarrassed by difficult or challenging experiences, as though this might allow us to push them away successfully. The outflowing, expressive form is anger; the frozen, inflowing form is fear. Both are striking out against what is happening, trying to separate from it, wanting to declare it to be untrue.

We can give ourselves permission to feel things. We begin to view our mind states almost like weather. We learn to take an interest in our passing storms rather than feeling so threatened by them. If we cultivate mindfulness, we learn to neither grab hold of these passing feelings, identifying with them, nor push them away. Instead, we recognize our reactions for what they are, with enough spaciousness to choose whether to act on them or let them go.

I am not suggesting that we talk ourselves out of our feelings, merely that it is skillful to remember we can be empowered to have a choice as to how we want to act on them. Maybe it's *Well, last time I exploded, it didn't work that well. This might be a good time to leave the room and come back later.*

We don't want to disparage any feeling; rather, we want to understand each of them, and have tools to relate to feelings differently, perhaps unconventionally. We want to elicit the gifts they may give us if we neither become defined by them nor make them an enemy and try to deny them.

In the case of aversion, in its angry form, the gift is the energy itself, which ensures that we're not passive or complacent. We're also not complicit. If we can utilize that energy and not get lost in the anger, we can have the courage to speak out—maybe pointing out problems no one else in the room cares to notice, let alone mention. There is a lot of strength there. But if we are *lost* in anger with no space at all, it is likened in Buddhist psychology to a forest fire, which burns up its own support. It can destroy the host: us. It can range wildly, leaving us far from where we want to be. The last several years I've found myself several times on a remote fire watch, concerned about friends in California, in Colorado, knowing people whose lives have been overturned, who have lost so much. Each time, I think about that metaphor. The skillful approach is not to be afraid of it but to learn how to cultivate some space.

Even when it is a low smolder, and yet pervasive, aversion can damage us. Think of the most chronically resentful person you know (and I find myself hoping, for your sake, it is not you yourself). But regardless of who it is, just spend a couple of minutes using active imagination, placing yourself solidly in that state. Feel how enclosed it is, cramped, constricted. When I do that exercise, I find my mind laced through with hopelessness, loneliness—not a very generative or supportive quality!

Having felt that quality of constriction viscerally, it helps to know that resentment doesn't have to be the steady state we cultivate, even if it might arise out of our conditioning. With greater mindfulness, we have alternative ways of working with all forms of aversion and a greater ability to capture the sheer energy of it in a more positive way.

One of the clearest domains to explore the difference between being able to channel the forceful, cutting-through energy of anger and being overwhelmed by it is the anger we direct at ourselves. This is the difference between, on the one hand, a clear-eyed self-assessment of where we might seek change, and, on the other hand, bullying ourselves.

OUR MISTAKES

MANY SYSTEMS of thought distinguish between having a conscience and engaging in a lacerating self-hatred that doesn't allow for change or growth. As individuals and members of a society, we need the former, because some kind of moral inventory of our speech and actions (and the times we have refrained from speaking or acting) is the basis for sensitivity, honor, and empathy. The self-hatred, by contrast, doesn't really do us any good. No one can be expected to make no mistakes. We can learn from our mistakes, though, and strengthen the intention not to repeat them.

In the language of Buddhist psychology, we would call the skillful development of conscience *remorse* and being stuck in castigating ourselves *guilt*. When we feel remorse, we are able to recognize personal responsibility, feel the pain of what we've done or said, allow ourselves to release it, and free the energy to move on. Guilt, however, is exhausting and doesn't leave us with the energy to change our lives. Instead, it leaves us constricted and seething, trapped in a coil of self-punishment.

In the language of Western psychology, it's expressed differently. *Guilt* (what I'm used to calling *remorse*) is "I did something wrong" versus *shame* (what I'm used to calling *guilt*) is "I am a bad person." So, in this system, when we feel guilty, there's actually a motivational aspect to try to create change, but with shame, there's not. Guilt (in the Western psychological language) can motivate us to act, make amends, or learn from our mistakes. Shame informs us that we ourselves are a mistake.

We become identified with our shame-making event, as if *that* is all we are or will ever be. Shame brings us right up to the line of believing we are worthless. Will we topple over and be trapped in that narrow and circumscribed view?

Here we can see a socially sanctioned manifestation of aversion toward ourselves, as though shame will lead to harmony and behavior change instead of just more hating on ourselves.

For happiness and freedom, it's good to keep our eyes on the prize . . . what we want is behavior change, so we can have a happier, more expansive life, and families, communities, organizations, and the world can be in less pain.

HEALING SHAME

ONE OF the last in-person gatherings I attended, prior to the COVID pandemic, was in 2020 in mid-February, on a trip to California. At that gathering, psychologist Eve Ekman said something I found fascinating:

The brain filled with shame cannot learn.

✳

Remember, we are looking toward behavior change, and learning is a crucial component of that. By mid-March I was in lockdown in Barre, Massachusetts, with more quiet time to myself, so I began studying more deeply how shame blocks learning.

Our lives change when we begin to ask ourselves: What would it be like to have a mind not so easily overwhelmed by harmful thoughts? A mind that does not disparage us in terms of our actions, speech, thoughts, desires, or fears—and does not deride others for these things either. A mind that is aware of the joy of committing to not causing harm yet realizes that love and compassion are better catalysts for change than shame or fear.

Nadia Bolz-Weber—an ordained Lutheran pastor and the founder of the House for All Sinners & Saints in Denver, Colorado—is the creator and host of the *Confessional* podcast, which invites guests to share stories about times they were at their worst. Among other books, Nadia is the author of *Pastrix: The Cranky, Beautiful Faith of a Sinner & Saint*. In 2021, she launched the Chapel, a yearlong project that served as a pop-up chapel for in-depth conversation, daily prayer, and community.

When I spoke with Nadia in 2021, she talked about the consequences of toxic shame:

Shame keeps us from being able to speak the truth about our failings. It keeps us from the truth of the ways maybe we haven't done something we should or we've done something we shouldn't have. I think of the story of Adam and Eve. It's interesting that they covered themselves because they were ashamed of their nakedness, but that was only after they listened to a voice that was not a divine voice tell them who they are.

And so God's like, "Hey, where are you guys hanging out?" and they're like, "Oh, we're scared of you and we're naked." And God's like, "Hold on, who told you you were naked?" Shame has an origin, and it isn't in the divine; it often originates in voices that claim they are speaking for God and they're not, or voices that are claiming an authority that they don't truly have. And so I've always wondered how the story would've ended differently if Adam and Eve just said, "Oh yeah, well, we did something you told us not to and now we kind of get it. Are we good?" And God's like, "Yeah, we're good."

But they couldn't do that. They couldn't just tell the truth; they had to blame other people, they had to lie, they had to hide, all of the things we do now as a result of shame. Shame makes us place blame on everything externally; it makes us not admit the truth. If freedom comes from some kind of truth about ourselves, shame will always obscure it—both the good and the bad. I wonder if when it comes to forgiving ourselves, if it's a little bit the same: if I can't forgive myself for mistakes I've made or things I've done or said or not done or said, I'm only seeing myself as that. I cannot let competing information enter that might be positive about who I am.

I appreciate Nadia's perspective on forgiveness, because it's a challenging concept. As Sylvia Boorstein once said to me, "Forgiveness is not amnesia." That's how most people take it, though. So, I've seen a number of cases where somebody chooses to move on but they don't like calling it *forgiveness*. When it comes to our own faults and our mistakes, we can learn to recount when we behaved badly without it threatening to destroy our self-esteem. Shame keeps us from being honest, but interconnectedness and belonging combat shame. We can connect to this by recognizing our own shame and sharing it. Shame grows in secrecy, so owning our story and recognizing our humanness can be healing, as if Adam and Eve just said, "Yes, we screwed up."

DELUSION

INTERESTINGLY, THE English word *delusion* comes from the Latin *deludere*—"to mock, to deceive." In Pali, the language of the original Buddhist texts, the word for *delusion* is *moha*, which means "to be stupefied." In everyday life, delusion is the feeling of being on the road and suddenly not knowing if you're in Massachusetts or New Jersey—maybe not sure where you're even going or why. Strong delusion we experience in the mind as confusion, bewilderment, dullness, helplessness.

These days, we'd commonly say, "I'm spaced out." We feel numb, cocooned in a fog, disconnected, and typically not caring that we're in this state. In fact, we might like it. When lost in the fog, we don't have to be too aware of discomfort.

DELUSION ENCOMPASSES:

- numbness to feelings;

- disembodiment; and

- holding on mightily to what we think might shelter us in the fog—such as rigidly insisting on one's unverified viewpoint, even to the point of fanaticism.

In some sense, delusion is a state of not realizing what we know, and what we don't know—while not actually asking the right questions. It is a state of failure or resistance to see things as they truly are.

But why?

Answer: uncertainty and confusion.

Instead of mindfully accepting difficult experiences, or being able to sit and face ambiguity, our uneasiness causes us to space out or become numb. Sometimes we have the habit of going into a deluded state whenever our experience is painful. We use spacing out as a method of self-protection. Delusion can also happen when our experience is fairly neutral. We may count on intensity, both pleasurable and painful, to feel alive.

When things are neutral, we often just want to take a nap. Or maybe the opposite—we feel the need to escape when it's all too intense. We might prefer to zone out, numbing ourselves through rumination or a mind-altering substance or simply by disassociating, to try to turn down the interior "noise" or wide-ranging emotional intensity.

Delusion has been my go-to place for a very long time. Beginning during the upheavals of my childhood, I've found distinct comfort in not feeling, solace in just kind of coasting along in a vague sort of way. While mindfulness practice has made a huge difference, my personality structure is such that long before grasping or aversion become predominant, I get to feel the subtle undertow of delusion beckoning me to drift away.

Delusion has the characteristic of not knowing what's going on. Its function is to conceal the true nature of things, and it manifests as darkness. One limiting constraint of being lost in delusion is that we end up relying on someone else's vision of what is true, rather than on our own direct perception. I often refer to something that happened to me years ago. One evening I left my home in Barre, Massachusetts, drove to Cambridge to give a talk, and drove home afterward. I parked my car outside my house and went to bed.

I woke up the next morning and walked the short distance to the Insight Meditation Society to teach. As I passed the spot where I'd parked the night before, I noticed my car was no longer there. I thought, *That's funny, my car's gone. Why is that? Maybe somebody took it to put gas in it.* I went into the center, and the first person I encountered was someone most likely to have taken the car to the gas station.

"Did you take my car?" I asked him.

"No, I didn't take your car."

"You *didn't?*" I was genuinely puzzled.

"No."

"Well, it's gone."

And then came the killer moment, when he asked me, "Are you sure?"

Am I sure? I mused. *It really seems to be gone. It looks gone.* Right away, though, I started to doubt myself. It took all morning to unwind what had happened: a staff member knew I would be teaching all day and lent it to someone else who had an emergency.

It's a simple story, but it remains a prime illustration of one of the dangers of delusion. We lose confidence in *our own perception of the truth,* we feel confused, and if things keep going, we might start getting awfully used to letting others lay claim to the truth.

FUNDAMENTALISM

WHEN WE don't quite know what's happening, we get uneasy. Because of that uneasiness, we look for something to hold on to. We might cling to rigid stories, views, assumptions, judgments, preconceptions—hoping they will provide a path out of the clouds. All of these responses, however, can in fact further obscure our vision and instead create misimpressions, illusions. This is the mind of dogmatism or fanaticism or conceit. It is as narrow a strait as one can imagine.

A common example used to illustrate this kind of delusion is being in the wilderness during a storm. If we can find anything that might provide us some kind of security, we'll hold on tightly to it. In the howling wind and exposed to the elements, we cling tenaciously, rigidly, to anything we can find that seems to offer certainty, and we will refuse to relinquish it.

But is it actually providing a refuge? Can we instead choose to navigate the storm? The more we practice paying attention, with balance, the more the clouds clear, the more we see and know. That clarity is our most reliable refuge.

THE WAY FORWARD

IN BUDDHIST TEACHING, the journey to freedom can be described as

> Moving from
>> craving / endless searching
>>> to
>>>> peace

> Moving from
>> aversion (anger and fear)
>>> to
>>>> compassion

> Moving from
>> delusion
>>> to
>>>> vibrancy and connection

And it is realizable. Even if we have strongly conditioned patterns, all is mutable. I remember my high school science education on genes and chromosomes. I found it fascinating, and at one point, I thought of becoming a geneticist. After I began meditating, I began to imagine that if the DNA code were a language, all expressions of DNA, including our lives themselves, would be a form of language. Our noses and bodies and diseases and proclivities and inclinations would all be language—not clunky, solid, oppressive things, impermeable, rigid, totally and absolutely determined, but flowing, translucent conversations.

Let's shape the conversation of our very existence into one that is about real freedom.

3

BEING WITH
DIFFICULT FEELINGS

✳

IN HER BOOK *Here If You Need Me,* Kate Braestrup—who serves as a chaplain to search and rescue workers in Maine—recounts being called out to sit with the parents of a missing six-year-old child (later found alive after many hours lost in the woods). The little girl's mother said to her, "It's so cool that the warden service has a chaplain to keep us from freaking out."

Braestrup responded, "I'm not really here to keep you from freaking out. I'm here to be with you *while* you freak out."

Braestrup knows that as a chaplain, it's not her job to take people's suffering away. Instead, she says, "I am there if they want to grieve or laugh or suffer or sing. It is a ministry of presence. It is showing up with a loving heart." She makes clear that it's not a magic wand. It's simply the most helpful and effective way to show up in the midst of an emotional maelstrom.

Many healing modalities, such as mindfulness meditation, are designed to help us cultivate a ministry of presence for ourselves—a council of forgiveness, compassion, and openness in the face of our own inner pain—so that ultimately, we are also relating differently to the pain of others. We effect change by profoundly transforming the environment the pain is held within.

We move from constriction to expansion not by demanding that a painful emotion just simply disappear, or by straining to change its nature, but by surrounding it with spaciousness—a spaciousness infused with kindness.

When I first began meditation practice, I was eighteen years old. Although I knew I was deeply unhappy, I wasn't aware of the separate threads of grief, anger, and fear at play inside me. Once I began practicing meditation, I started to look within more clearly and to detect the various components of my sorrow. What I saw unsettled me so much that at one point I marched up to my teacher, S. N. Goenka, and said accusingly, "I never used to be an angry person before I began meditating!"

Of course, I had been quite angry. I felt abandoned—by my mother dying when I was a child, by my father disappearing, by the world itself, since I felt so different from those around me. The introspection of meditation started allowing me to uncover the strands of that pain. When I blamed my teacher, Mr. Goenka, and meditation itself for causing my pain, he simply laughed. Then, he reminded me of the tools I now had to deal with the difficult feelings I used to keep hidden, even from myself. I could begin to forge a new relationship with my emotions—to find the vital middle place between denying them and being overwhelmed by them.

At first, I was frightened and disturbed, until I recalled a meditation instruction that set me down a particular path:

Practice looking directly at difficult feelings, and practice having equanimity, or peace of mind, toward them.

When I encountered it, I kept thinking, *That's ridiculous. What good is looking directly at these difficult feelings going to do? That makes no sense. What does it even mean? I'm trapped. There is no way out.*

The suffering simply increased.

But at one point, with little confidence the story would have a happy ending, little trust the approach was likely to work, I tried it. And to my surprise, because I wasn't so busy pushing away the challenging feelings, I could begin to discern the different strands that were defining my relationship to these feelings:

- shame (*I'm not worthy of thinking I could feel better*)

- self-judgment (*I should have been able to stop this pattern long ago*)

- fear (*I don't care what it takes; I have to avoid this*)

- overidentification (*This is who I am fundamentally; it will never change*)

- isolation (*I'm the only one to feel this so acutely; no one could ever understand me*)

These habits cluttered up the available space in my heart and mind. Nowadays, that clutter reminds me of space debris, material orbiting Earth that is no longer functional—sometimes as large as a discarded rocket stage, sometimes as small as a microscopic chip of paint. Apparently, there's a lot of it, and it's moving very quickly.

At some point, the add-ons—like shame and fear—probably were useful in some way. Not allowing ourselves to feel an emotion or more fully inhabit our bodies, for example, might have been smart survival tools at some point, but now, like a discarded piece of equipment, they may not be so functional anymore. Therefore, encountering them, we work to recognize them, to forgive ourselves for what we're feeling, to see more deeply into the heart of the feelings, and to not identify with them as fundamentally, essentially who we are.

Some of you might recognize the practice of RAIN in that formula:

R for recognize,

A for allow,

I for investigate, and

N for non-identify.

RAIN was first coined by meditation teacher Michele McDonald. Another colleague, Tara Brach, has popularized the use of RAIN and tends these days to describe the *N* as nurturing—remembering to be kind to yourself. The use of RAIN shows us how we might create a larger, lighter, kinder space for any emotion, so that our sense of who we are is not fused with or defined by our emotions. This brings about a natural sense of greater freedom and ease. That is the internal ministry of presence.

It's also important to challenge the habit of consolidating our emotional experience—projecting what we are feeling into the next two or ten years and trying to work it all out *right now*, instead of just dealing with what actually *is* right now. This dissipates a great deal of the strength and confidence we could be feeling by agglomerating the minute feelings of the moment into a monumental lifelong big deal.

I remember teaching at the Insight Meditation Society (IMS) with a colleague, Susan O'Brien. Susan had started her meditation practice at IMS about fifteen years earlier, and I had been one of her first teachers. I was listening to Susan give the evening discourse one day, when I heard her tell this story:

> During my first retreat I went through a bout of restlessness so intense I thought I was going to jump out of my skin. So I went to Sharon and asked, "Has anyone ever died of restlessness doing meditation practice?"

Naturally, I was really eager to hear what I had said all those many years ago, and I leaned forward in my seat. Susan went on:

> And Sharon replied, "Not from just one moment at a time of it."

Good answer! I thought.

SHAKE HANDS

TIBETAN TEACHER Tsoknyi Rinpoche, author of *Open Heart, Open Mind: Awakening the Power of Essence Love,* among many other books, shares a way of connecting to ourselves called the *handshake practice.* In it, we are invited to shake hands with what he calls "our beautiful monsters." To start with he says, "Come into your body. Don't look for special things, just be with what's there. No need to impress anyone, or impress me. Just be honest with yourself, be with yourself, with whatever is there. Be kind to your phenomena. Every feeling is priceless."

Instead of running from these beautiful monsters, we begin to shake hands with them. "For each of us, they will be different, but we all have them. If you don't have them," Rinpoche quips, "you're not normal."

The four ways of being that make for skillful handshaking are:

1. **Soften and allow** for your experience; no need to suppress or push down what's arising. Like a beach ball being pushed underwater, the force it's pushed down with is the same pressure it will shoot back up with.

2. **Stay grounded,** and instead of adding logs to the fire and creating more flames, settle back. This means not indulging whatever comes up, becoming swept away.

3. **Be with yourself** without expecting to change what's here. There's a kindness in just being with. We can sense, even if it's subtle: "I'm going to transform you!"

4. **Listen and welcome.** Instead of ignoring or dismissing, we give the gift of our attention.

We practice this not for the sake of being overwhelmed by distressing feelings or giving in to damaging patterns. Rather, we do it for the simple reason that if we can begin with more spaciousness in our minds toward what we're feeling, we can be less afraid, less driven unthinkingly into any old way of finding relief. Expansiveness, spaciousness, allows options for going forward to appear. Creativity now has some room to arise. We're grounded more in love for ourselves than in belittlement. It's not that we never do anything about conditions in our lives, never exercise real and practical and committed efforts to work for change, but we don't need to act driven by a belief that we can't possibly face the truth of the moment.

I remember a time when someone I knew became very ill and subsequently died. He was a much-loved person, so it was strange to see, after his death, members of his larger circle turning on each other, fighting about all kinds of things, threatening lawsuits. I was bemused, when someone closer to those involved said to me, "I think none of us knows how to grieve." It was a good point and a reflection I've taken with me as I've witnessed families and workplaces (and these days, it seems, whole countries) meet severe adversity. In the wake of loss and amid seemingly insurmountable obstacles, spaciousness is at a premium, and yet it is the very thing we need.

Being with difficult feelings with spaciousness also demands wisdom and self-knowledge. For example, we don't try to shake hands with our beautiful monsters unremittingly. Sometimes we're tired. We need to rest or lighten the load we carry. Sometimes we really need a break, and we would benefit from placing our attention elsewhere, someplace that soothes or nourishes us.

For intensive retreats at IMS, the suggested guidelines include, whenever possible, using that period as a time to not be on the phone with friends or family, except in cases of emergency. During one such retreat, one of my students didn't follow through on that and made a surprise call home. What she discovered indicated the unexpected end of her marriage. In shock, she came to tell me. We still see each other occasionally, now many years later (and let me say she is tremendously happy in her new life). She laughs as she recounts what happened next: "I told you what had happened, I saw your eyes open very wide, and you silently got up, went into the bathroom, and came back with this big bottle of bubble bath, saying, 'First I want you to go take a bubble bath. We'll talk later.'"

Sometimes we feel we sorely lack perspective. We need to go outside and look at the sky or touch a tree. We can also learn to employ diverse conceptual frameworks that help us view our experience from different angles. I was once at a lecture about trauma and its effects on the nervous system, including the vagus nerve, that reflected a current view of one way traumatic experience might linger within us and how we can approach healing. A woman accompanying me had some years before lost her son to gun violence. Because of her religious background, she felt obligated to come to a view that cast the immense tragedy in the light of "God's will," which she absolutely could not do. Therefore, not only was she suffering the pain of that tragedy, but she was also suffering estrangement from the reality of what she was feeling, in deference to an ideal she could not seem to attain. I witnessed her having many theological arguments with herself and her friends, and I saw that she was very down on herself. After the lecture, she turned to me, and to my surprise (the lecture had been quite scientific and rather long), she was radiant. She said, "It's not my lack of appropriate faith; it's my nervous system!"

Sometimes more than anything, we need to focus on loving ourselves no matter what, because otherwise we're continually sitting in judgment of ourselves and adding pain to pain. On my podcast, *Metta Hour,* I asked meditation teacher Sebene Selassie, author of *You Belong: A Call to Connection,* about this habit of harsh self-judgment and how to respond with love. She replied:

> Yeah, someone was asking me about this when we were talking about shame, and they said, "So I'm supposed to

love my shame?" It's not the patterns—especially the un-skillful patterns—that we're trying to release, the ones that are harmful to us or to others, but it's really loving ourselves before that conditioning.

And seeing that those patterns, that conditioning, that unconscious material and the behaviors that come out of it, that's not what we're loving. We're loving ourselves despite the fact that we're caught in that conditioning.

That took me a really long time to grok and to be able to, whenever I see them, really just put a hand on my heart and say to myself, *Oh yeah, okay, I see that, and I love you despite these things that are covering over that true belonging that's there.*

Sometimes we may need to pace back and forth or run or move really quickly to discharge some pent-up energy. Sometimes we need to reach out to someone to hear their faith in us or simply to be reminded that spaciousness and love exist. Sometimes we may need to cry. Some years after my first retreat, during an intensive retreat at IMS, I was studying with a Burmese monastic teacher, Sayadaw U Pandita. A few months before, a close friend had died by suicide, and I was deeply saddened. Still, I was somewhat re-luctant to let myself share the extent of this with such a revered teacher. In my mind, I saw Sayadaw U Pandita as an ascetic who had left the world of messy emotions behind.

One day during a regularly scheduled personal meeting, after I told him about my sadness, he asked me if I'd been crying.

I tried to contour my response to what I thought he'd want to hear. "Just a little bit," I said.

His reply shocked me: "Every time you cry, you should cry your heart out. That way, you'll get the best release."

Eventually, the sadness moved through me. It was a feeling that needed to be honored—and once I allowed it more fully, I was no longer held captive by it.

And if we are confused, overwhelmed, if we can't sense what approach to try even as an experiment, that's when we can rely on mentors, or therapists, or meditation teachers, or a community.

The point of our efforts is not to suffer on and on, or re-traumatize ourselves. The light we discover, the space we can breathe more freely within, is a reflection of an innate capacity available to us—one that is all too often unrealized.

IN THE WINDOW

THE ABILITY to create a context of feeling more balanced, grounded, clear, safe, and present in relationship to whatever difficult emotion may be presenting itself reminds me of psychiatrist Dan Siegel's formulation of the *window of tolerance*.

This is a phrase used to describe our mind/body reactions, especially when confronting something challenging. It suggests that we have an optimal, calm arousal level when we are within our window of tolerance. That allows for the ups and downs of emotions we experience within a context made up of the qualities listed previously: greater safety, presence, balance, and so forth. However, when we become overstimulated from fear or pain or pressure to the degree that it pushes us outside of our window of tolerance, we enter *hyperarousal*.

Hyperarousal is characterized by states such as anxiety, panic, fear, hypervigilance, and emotional flooding. Its opposite, *hypoarousal*, also might occur when we have moved too much into *hyper*arousal, surpassing the sense of overwhelm our mind/body is able to tolerate, causing us to move into a state of shutting down.

It's characterized by exhaustion, numbness, disconnection, dissociation, and the like.

Hyperarousal resembles the fight/flight end of the spectrum of the stress response dynamic. We're stuck "in a high." Hypoarousal resembles the tendency toward freezing, from that same dynamic. We're stuck "in a low." Neither is aligned with integration, with the wholeness of our being.

All of us leave that window of tolerance, sometimes frequently. As we grow in awareness, we learn about our own tendencies toward dysregulation, and what it feels like when we've left our window. One pole of dysregulation is sometimes described as chaos, the other as rigidity. We can feel these in our bodies, in our minds. We can see them in our energy levels, in our engagement with or disavowal of life. We can recognize the hypervigilance or the numbness. If we understand what is happening, it's not a cause for judgment. Instead of thinking of ourselves as bad or wrong, we recognize that we're out of balance. We can learn approaches to help ease hyperarousal or wake up from hypoarousal—approaches that help us come back into balance by addressing body, mind, and spirit.

TOOL KIT

WE CAN become aware when we're hyper and pick up tools to find greater ease. We can become aware when we feel distant from life, cut off, and pick up tools to more strongly connect. These tools can also become a more regular part of our everyday experience, to support us as a kind of scaffolding even *before* we might come to notice bigger swings of dysregulation. In a podcast interview with me, Zainab Salbi, whom we met in chapter 1, told me about *her* tool kit:

I have my seven rules for a happy day. Perhaps it's not happiness per se, because happiness is an exaggerated promise. For me, it's contentment.

A happy day for me is:

1. Drink lots of water.

2. Eat healthy food.

3. Make "an appointment with your heart." I really abide by that. I go and meet with my heart.

4. Be in the presence of nature, which when I'm in a city might simply mean touching a tree somewhere.

5. Do something in the arts. Anything. For example, recently I retaught myself to play piano. I can do that, even if it's just for ten minutes.

6. Connect with family and friends.

7. Live your purpose. I fulfill my purposes for that day, and they're very basic: all of the above.

That is my happy day.

Obviously, it's impossible sometimes to do all of this, but at least enough of them are happening that I'm okay. I can carry myself through—because our fullness does not betray us, nor does it betray others, nor does it betray our cause. It is our scarcity that betrays.

It's a useful exercise to periodically consider what tools would be on your own list of seven or five or three rules for your own happy day. Maybe it's remembering to breathe. Move your body. Look at the sky.

Whatever these may be for any of us, we can commit to a short period of putting those into practice (remember, no judgment if it's quite short), so they leave the realm of abstraction and ideals and become tangible. Then, we can recognize what we are truly feeling, in our bodies, minds, and spirits in the moment.

WIDENING THE RIVER

EVEN AS we learn more and more how to come back into balance, our journey of moving from constriction to expansion is ultimately realized by widening the window of tolerance. Our aim is to essentially broaden this window and increase our capacity to hold emotional experiences (even intense ones) without their landing us in a state of either chaos or rigidity. That space in the middle is where discomfort can arise but does not become all-consuming, either through our identification with it or our strident efforts to reject it.

We can also picture the window of tolerance as a river. We're floating down the middle of that river. When we expand our window of tolerance, the river widens and the flow slows down. We feel more comfortable, safer, streaming down the waters. We see the shoals, we perceive the eddies, we recognize the signs of danger, but we have room to move.

However, when we're exhausted or feel a big burden of undue stress, when we have little confidence or sense of support, our window of tolerance likely shrinks, and the river begins to narrow and speed up. As it tightens into twisty, narrow channels and rapids, we relate to the potential obstacles we are seeing with more and more anxiety, more dread; all around us, danger seems heightened. We feel more uncomfortable, less safe, and have more difficulty keeping afloat.

If we need to, we can remind ourselves that there are islands along that river. We can stop and take a moment, remember to breathe, to put into practice any tools of balance we have been cultivating.

That's never wrong.

✳

Every time we're working to establish a different, more open, more loving context within which our emotional lives can exist, we are widening that window.

The handshake practice is one way.

All the different elements of RAIN are also useful. To review, they are:

R *for recognize*—Notice the predominant emotion in your emotional landscape. Is it reflected in sensations in your body? What is your sense of the emotion? Some research suggests that mentally labeling an emotion gives us more perspective on it, helping us move from "I *am* angry. That's who I *am*" to "I am *feeling* anger." In other words, we recognize what's happening but with more space.

A *for allow*—We can look for the add-ons—perhaps shame about what we are feeling, or hardening resistance to it—that have joined the emotion, and see if we can relinquish them.

I *for investigate*—Bring a quality of interest and curiosity to your experience: "What am I experiencing in my body right now? What's happening as the jealousy/anger/fear movie unfolds? What other emotions are held within the primary one?"

N *for non-identify*—When experiencing a challenging emotion, we often feel strangely unique. It's helpful to remind ourselves that whatever we are feeling is a part of common human experience. We can also remind ourselves of our own innate power of awareness, which doesn't need to be subsumed even by intense feeling. I saw an anecdote on Twitter the other day, which encapsulated this wisdom: journalist Megan K. Stack tweeted, "At bedtime the 8 yo told me his teacher said: 'Think of your mind like a pond full of fish and each fish is a feeling. Try to be the pond, not the fish.' And all I can say is primary school has significantly improved."

Alternatively, N *for nurture*—No matter what is happening, the bottom line is practicing kindness toward yourself. Always.

Consolidating all that we are feeling and then projecting it onto a future we imagine as unchanging inevitably leads us to experience overwhelm. By contrast, no matter what the emotion is, when we remember to deal with one moment at a time of it, we become empowered.

Because my own go-to place when experiencing a challenging emotion is to feel abandoned, left to deal with it all alone, I have a practice of calling in the forces of good. I recollect my own courageous and loving teachers, the generations of people who have sought freedom whose lineages I am a part of, those I admire who are showing up to serve in this world today. My heart expands, my perspective opens. The dimensions of that window shift right away.

WHAT DOES IT LOOK LIKE WHEN WE'VE WIDENED THE WINDOW OF TOLERANCE?

- We may be filled with fear and discover we can love ourselves anyway.

- We may have anger pouring through our bodies, while steering clear of either trying to push it way down deep never to be seen again or becoming consumed by it so that it takes over our day, perhaps our tomorrow and beyond.

- We may deeply grieve the loss of a person, or a situation, or our dreams and not deny how much we are hurting, while also holding close the ability to care that the grief represents.

- We may experience the intensity and pain of a reaction to something, and not confuse that with the crushing notion that we are all alone.

GRIEF

THE SATIRICAL late-night television host Stephen Colbert is the youngest of eleven children. He lost his two older brothers who were closest in age to him, Paul and Peter, and his father, James Colbert Jr., when they died in a plane crash on September 11, 1974. Colbert was ten years old.

Also at age ten, journalist and television host Anderson Cooper lost his father, Wyatt Cooper, who died during open-heart surgery. Ten years later, he lost his brother, Carter, who was two years older than Cooper, when Carter died by suicide by jumping from the fourteenth-floor terrace of his mother's New York City apartment. His mother, Gloria Vanderbilt, died in the summer of 2019. After hearing of Vanderbilt's passing, Colbert wrote to Cooper, saying, "I hope you find peace in your grief." This led to a connection over their shared loss and ultimately to a very vulnerable interview. I found this section that centered on the question "What do you get from experiencing loss?" especially moving and insightful:

Colbert: You get awareness of other people's loss, which allows you to connect with that other person, which allows you to love more deeply and to understand what it is like to be a human being, if it is true that all humans suffer. And however imperfectly, acknowledge their suffering and to connect with them and to love them in a deep way. It's about the fullness of your humanity.

Cooper: One of the things my mom would often say is, "I never ask 'Why me?'" She would always say, "Why not me?" Why would I be exempt from what has befallen countless others over the centuries? I think that's another thing that has helped me think, yes, of course, why not me? This is part of being alive. This is the suffering, you know, the sadness, suffering, you can't have happiness without having loss and suffering.

Stephen Colbert went on to talk about seeing suffering as a gift, saying it is a gift to realize we are so completely a part of life, to find ourselves in the experience of another, to know down to our bones that we are not stranded or alone.

I have known people who have genuinely come to see things this way and have also known people who have used that idea of suffering as a gift to bludgeon themselves for not being "spiritual" enough or "evolved" enough for that to be their experience. I appreciate Zen teacher Roshi Joan Halifax's challenge to the ways we might possibly misuse that idea: referring to childhood traumas, she said, "Think of them as givens, not gifts."

That way there's no pressure to conform to an idealistic notion. If something is a given, we work (sometimes slowly) to relax the grip of denying it or looking the other way. We acknowledge what we feel as fully as we can, and as our perception moves and shifts, layers upon layers will be revealed. The extant, shining heart of love at the core of grief can be recovered amid its lashings. Then we can see how we can have the best life possible going forward.

Psychiatrist Mark Epstein has said, "Grief and love are connected. If we push the mourning, the grief, the sadness away, we are also pushing the love away. By doing so, we are creating a much more constrained way of living."

It's important to remember we are not in a contest; there is no pass/fail, there's no grading on how you are handling your life.

Sometimes painful feelings are just too overwhelming for us to experiment much with. Broadening the context within which we're viewing them may be an effort perhaps best suited to another day. As groundbreaking educator and activist Parker Palmer, author of more than ten books, notes in reference to depression, "Sometimes . . . we become the darkness." If that's the case right now, hopefully we can hang in there and not give up on ourselves. All things do shift and change.

To the extent that we can open our hearts to ourselves and what we are feeling, we encounter a more complete aliveness—tender, vibrant, precious—that has been, for many of us, long hidden from expression. We encounter an ability to be more fully present, not based on the exhilaration of accumulating accomplishments or fulfilling our desires. We encounter a capacity to live in a way that is more direct and real. We encounter a vulnerability that joins us to others, so we know we are not so alone. We encounter a power of love nestled nascent within us, just waiting for conditions to come together for it to spring forth. As Victor Bucklew, author of *The Hidden Gifts of Addiction,* said so beautifully,

Through finally meeting our inner experiences with honesty and love, we may notice a sense of ourselves that is deeper than any story, emotion, or thought that we may be having. We may notice whether the part that has let go has opened up space for recognizing what has always been here. And once opened, the connection with the presence of this moment, a deeper aspect of who we are, always remains. It is this aspect of ourselves that is innately healing.

4

THE LIGHT WITHIN

✳

I N SO MANY WAYS, when we look toward a more open, expansive environment from which we can transform our relationship to life, we are looking at love. In a 2000 interview with the National Public Radio program *All Things Considered,* the late writer and activist bell hooks spoke about the life-changing power of love—that is, the act of loving and how love is far broader than romantic sentiment:

I'm talking about a love that is transformative, that challenges us in both our private and our civic lives . . . Everywhere I go, people want to feel more connected. They want to feel more connected to their neighbors. They want to feel more connected to the world. And when we learn that through love we can have that connection, we can see the stranger as ourselves. And I think that it would be absolutely fantastic to have that sense of "Let's return to kind of a utopian focus on love, not unlike the sort of hippie focus on love." Because I always say to people, you know, the '60s focus on love had its stupid sentimental dimensions, but then it had these life-transforming dimensions.

I had met bell by the time of that interview, and we had become friends. I told her I was a bona fide former hippie—in fact, I had been to Woodstock. The idea that the North Star of a society (or a group, or a family) could be love, not war, was important for me and transformative. It ultimately led me to India and a personal and direct exploration of love in the form of lovingkindness meditation.

Although love is almost always referred to as an emotion, sometimes even as the supreme emotion, I generally try these days to draw a bigger picture of love—one where it might sometimes appear as conventionally emotional, and at other times, it might not appear in that way at all. Both can be powerful.

To me, for example, inclusion looks like a face of love. We might realize we haven't been fully present with someone because of distraction, or an assumption about them as not worth much of our time, or perhaps simply because of bad habits of attention. When we become aware of not really being present or open and gather our attention to more completely see someone and hear what they're saying, that is a gesture of love.

I see recognizing our existence as interdependent as a face of love. This isn't the same thing as liking each other; it is a realization that our lives are inextricably interwoven. Then perhaps we take a moment to thank someone or hold them in appreciation. I remember, in the height of the pandemic in 2020, speaking to the head of a large medical practice at a hospital and hearing him say, "You know who I have a whole new appreciation for? The cleaning staff." And I thought, *Well, yes!* We might be reluctant to think of that kind of appreciation as love, but a recognition of interdependence can go bone-deep and also counts as love. It counts in an important way, because it transforms our worldview.

Can we see each moment as expressive of those who have influenced us, a confluence of impressions and relationships and connections? Can we find ourselves in one another?

I think about the face of love that recognizes suffering: compassion. In compassion, love is laced through with tenderness and with poignancy rather than exhilaration: "Would that I could just go *poof* and relieve you of all pain. But life just isn't like that." This may not be highly emotional, yet it is love, and even more specifically, love supported by wisdom.

While judgment is monolithic and fixed, compassion is complex and expansive, an evolving part of a living system. It accommodates the reality that we operate within the fragility of life, the difficult transfer of intention to impact, and personal imperfection in nearly every moment of the day. We see we can open to suffering—our own and others'—without getting engulfed by it, and we see that, despite strategies and plans and tactics, loving presence is the most healing force of all.

Several years ago, I was teaching in New York City and scheduled to have dinner with a friend farther uptown that night. With the teaching behind me, in the cab heading to her apartment,

I got a message from my friend saying she wasn't feeling well and thought we should skip it. I asked the cabdriver to turn around and head downtown. Writing back to my friend, I let her know that I was sorry that she was feeling ill, and I said something like, "There seem to be big germs around these days."

She responded, "Oh, it's nothing physical. Something painful happened to me today, and I didn't want to ruin your evening by my feeling down."

I replied, "I'm a Buddhist. I'm not brought down by someone's suffering." With her assent, our plans were on again. I felt rather dramatic, like a character in an old cops-and-robbers movie, saying to the cabdriver, "Turn around. We're going uptown!"

My friend and I spent a simple, undramatic evening together.

As we open to one another in compassion, we see that we needn't feel so cut off and alone, that in truth the fundamental nature of reality is that we all belong. We can find a home in this body, this mind, with one another, on this planet. To drive home this point, Sebene Selassie likes to quote the late Zen teacher Charlotte Joko Beck, who said, "Joy is exactly what's happening, minus our opinion of it. . . . This is freedom. Love is the ultimate expression of joy and freedom. Joy, freedom, and love could be considered synonyms for each other, and for belonging."

I consider love a basis for courageous action, in whatever scope—person to person, in one's family, in one's community. It isn't sappy, pretentious, or hell-bent on avoiding honesty and challenge.

I often think of this quotation from progressive Christian author Rachel Held Evans: "Imagine if every church became a place where everyone is safe, but no one is comfortable. Imagine if every church became a place where we told one another the truth. We might just create sanctuary."

And by extension, imagine every home, classroom, workplace . . .
transformed to be a refuge of maximum growth *and* maximum
safety, supported by the force of love.

✳

In that same interview with *All Things Considered* that I mentioned
at the start of this chapter, bell hooks spoke about how love can be
the root of active engagement, as a catalyst for positive change:

> I'm so moved often when I think of the civil rights move-
> ment, because I see it as a great movement for social jus-
> tice that was rooted in love and that politicized the notion
> of love, that said, real love will change you.

HOW TO DEFINE LOVE

IN 1976, researchers Ellen Langer and Judith Rodin conducted
an experiment, giving houseplants to two groups of nursing-home
residents. They told half of these elderly people that the plants were
theirs to care for: they had to pay close attention to their plants'
needs for water and sunlight, and they had to respond carefully to
those needs. The researchers told the other half of the residents
that their plants were theirs to enjoy, but that they did *not* have to
take care of them; the nursing staff would care for the plants.

At the end of a year, the researchers compared the two groups
of elders. The residents who had been asked to care for their plants
were living longer than the norm, were much healthier, and were
more oriented toward and connected to their world. The other
residents, those who had plants but did not have to stay responsive
to them, simply reflected the norms for people their age in longev-
ity, health, alertness, and engagement with the world.

There were other day-to-day events where some of the residents were given choices and some control over decisions and others were not. The study has usually been described as being about choice and control. From the first time I heard of it, though, I thought of it as being about the enlivening power of connection, of loving attention, of caring.

It seems that plants and people share similar traits when it comes to surviving and flourishing. You can go into most any plant store and ask for plants for your home that will survive with very little attention. Spider plants, aloe vera, ZZ plants, and many succulents famously survive a great deal of neglect. People go on long vacations and find these plants living when they return, while all the others have died off. Of course, if you do decide to give these plants some attention, they will not just survive. They will flourish.

I most often think about love as an embodied knowing of connection—with ourselves, with one another, with life. At times it is expressive, at times wordless. Love is a resonance of the soul, lifting us out of the confining circumstances of the day, charging the moment with energy, and reinforcing our sense of belonging.

I see it as a connection that is alive and responsive: our hearts tremble or we have a clear intuition as to how the conversation may look from someone else's perspective, or we recognize for a moment that this person wants to be happy just as we do, that they have their own story and hopes and fears and dreams. We're naturally moved to wish they could have happiness and the causes of happiness (which are not necessarily what we have been taught they are), that they be free of suffering and its causes.

I'm trying to steer clear of the word *responsibility*, though that word would commonly be used in the story of the elderly taking care of their plants. Responsibility, for me, can get confused at times with co-dependency, with trying to be in control of what we could never control, with leaving ourselves out of the possibility of freedom. Sometimes we mistake excessive sacrifice for love, or martyrdom for generosity. Caring for ourselves is not in the picture. Then what we are feeling is more a distortion of love—maybe obligation, or over-idealism, or pressure—even as we yearn underneath for the genuine freedom and openness we sense we are capable of.

That reminds me of the Disney animated movie *Encanto*, where one of the characters, an older sister named Luisa, has Herculean strength. For a while in the movie, she's seen lifting pianos in one hand, dragging around houses, lifting groups of donkeys as though they were feathers. After a series of events, Luisa admits that, inwardly, she is breaking under the pressure. Because she was so strong, she shouldered more than her fair share of the burden and felt responsible for keeping things the same as they had been for everyone else. I considered her depiction later in the movie, when she could barely get off the couch, the breakthrough of the inner Luisa!

Don't you find the phrases *feel responsible for* and *be in control of* can get mixed up, much to our sorrow in this out-of-control world?

LOVE AND THRIVING

PLEASE REMEMBER that the way I'm using *contraction* refers to when we're fixated or have tunnel vision, when we're clinging or grasping or deeply afraid. *Expansion* is when we feel connected to a bigger world, we see options, we have more perspective, we have openness. The poet Rumi describes it this way: "There is one way of breathing that is shameful and constricted. Then, there's another way: a breath of love that takes you all the way to infinity."

When we use the word *love*, though, we might mean many

different things. I recorded a podcast with Omid Safi, a teacher in the Sufi tradition of *radical love,* and the founder of Illuminated Courses and Tours. He is a professor at Duke University, specializing in Islamic spirituality and contemporary thought. Here is some of what he had to say about love.

Radical love is a love that covers all, right? The snow doesn't say, "I'm going to fall on the house but not on the tree. I'm going to fall on the road but not on this bush." No, it generously covers everything. Everything looks beautiful covered in it and we can go out there in the crisp air and take a breath. As the breath enters us and fills our hearts and our lungs and our chests and then returns to the open air, we feel a sense of communion. That we are not cut off from nature, that at least for that moment, we're able to experience the sense of being at one with this air of love, this ocean of love we're walking in, swimming in, breathing in.

Just as we don't want love to become so individualized, so sexualized, so restricted to the realm of the physical that we are cut off from that vastness, we also don't want compassion and love and tenderness and mercy to be purely individual acts. They are also communal. This deep love, this compassion, radiates out like the sun. It has to.

Which connects me back to that radical love notion. The word *radical* originally had to do with being rooted. I love the idea that every tree needs to have roots that anchor it, that help it draw up nourishment and sustenance. We are like that tree, and we also grow and we expand our branches, heavenward, and we might provide shade and fruit far beyond where our roots are. There's something to that metaphor of remaining rooted, while reaching far beyond that original site.

One summer I was sitting with my newborn in that sacred place where the waves of the ocean were coming up to the sand and then receding. I held her in my lap very carefully and let the waves come and wash from our toes to our knees to our thighs, and then go back into the ocean. I wanted her to experience that.

Sitting there, I felt so connected to the ocean. It is made out of water, and I'm made out of water, and the water that makes me has also come from the ocean. All of a sudden, death was not so frightening. There was a time that the water in me came from the ocean. And now it has found life inside of me, and there will come a time that life will go back to the ocean. And there was a time that the dust, the soil, the clay of my body, came from faraway stars. Every mineral in our bodies comes from the stars, and reminds us that we are also celestial beings. And the time will come when it will go back there, star to star, earth to earth.

At this point in my life, maybe sitting by an ocean is when I experience radical love and radical amazement most. For somebody, that experience might come in meditation, or in prayer, or in reading Rumi. I suggest we find whatever practice nurtures us at the most radical level, the most rooted level, and return to that practice again and again and again, until it becomes a habit.

We went on to talk about how radical love might not have many conditions and strings attached—such as, *I will love a child so long as they grow up to fulfill my dreams for them*—but it rightfully has boundaries.

Growing up as an immigrant child, I have found that considering the strings that can be attached to love is not an abstract exercise. We are raised with a massive amount of sacrifice and love, and also the culture of guilt and shame of "your parents sacrifice for you, so you'd better be a doctor." The question of the difference between conditional and unconditional love is really important, then. And the purest of loves is a little bit like sunshine, or rainfall, or snowfall—simply covering.

There is a caveat, though, something that in this new decade of my life, I'm learning to sit with. And I'm curious about where it's going to go, because it doesn't come from my beloved Sufi books. It comes from listening to my friends and learning from their lived experience and wisdom. A lot of it comes from women, who talk about during how much of their life they've scattered their heart energy by giving of themselves and giving of themselves for others without necessarily being cared for in return. So, in this new phase of life, I'm also learning to value not so much the conditional nature of love but the understanding that love does come with boundaries, and those boundaries are also really important.

My Sufi sources took certain boundaries for granted, living in a world where social boundaries and etiquettes tended to be universally practiced, so they didn't feel the need to articulate them. In today's world, though, sometimes it can be a protection that needs to be explicitly pointed to. Radical love cannot be imposed, either. You constantly have to make space for people to explore their own reaction to the teachings you're sharing with them. It's important to have each person explore—whether through journaling, or sitting in silence, meditation, and reflection—what is it that feeds their soul.

In some cases in the Buddhist tradition, something might be implicit that we may need to make explicit, so that someone doesn't try to twist themselves into becoming something they're not to conform. In some cases, though, the teaching provides explicit instruction that can be a tremendous aid. For example, in formal lovingkindness practice, you begin by offering lovingkindness to *yourself* before offering it to anybody else. The underlying principle is that we do that practice in the easiest way possible, and you yourself are considered to be the easiest, the nearest at hand, and are as worthy of your own loving care as anybody else. And that serves as a foundation.

Clearly, lovingkindness for ourselves is not always the easiest, by any means, and I always urge people to go back to that underlying principle and just switch the order. It's not a problem. Though we may need flexibility, the lovingkindness instructions are quite explicit. We *have to* include ourselves at some point. Even as we may be cultivating enormous care and compassion for others, there needs to be a part of us that is not abandoning ourselves. There is a kind of profound equality of us and other people.

A greater understanding of the quality of equanimity, too, brings a kind of healthy boundary: *I will help you, my friend whom I love. You're having such a hard time, and I will do anything. But I'm actually not in control of the universe. This is out of my hands, ultimately.*

That attitude is in no way cold or withdrawing. Through the

wisdom of equanimity, it describes a natural boundary that needs to be there, which I think is the very boundary Omid is pointing to. Otherwise, we may end up acting not from generosity of spirit but from a kind of martyrdom, which is a very different kind of action.

More than anything, I think of love as an intentional practice. For me, that means every day, not out of compulsion or the need to fulfill a duty but for deepening joy. I work on paying more full attention; feeling and showing appreciation; recognizing someone's pain and responding to it with presence, even—and maybe especially—when I don't have a clue as to how to fix it. You might consider taking some time and experimenting with lovingkindness meditation (see the meditation guide in the appendix on page 176). As bell hooks has said, "love is a practice, and like most things we practice, it is difficult. That truth contrasts with everyone thinking love is easy, but what about when we encounter people we don't want to love? There are times I get up in the morning, and I think, 'Okay. Who am I to love today?' That is not a choice based on who I think is cute, or who I want to spend time with, but it's the recognition of the hunger we all have for love."

THE LIGHT WITHIN US ALL

THE WORD *tejas* from Pali, the language of the original Buddhist texts, has many meanings. It can mean "heat" or "flame" or "fire" or "light," and it also has a sense of "splendor" and "radiance" and "glory." *Tejas* is brightness, a potent and alive energy, a strength and power of luminosity. As we uncover it, *tejas* drives us toward life, openness, and renewal. This light exists nestled within us, innate to our beings, not because we are particularly unique or outstanding, or did something special to deserve it, but simply because we exist. Easily overlooked, often mistrusted, it is there. It's always there.

In a way, this journey from a narrow place to expansion and freedom lies outside of time and space. We can traverse that seemingly daunting distance with a thought. We can travel that length without accruing any mileage at all, with remembering right now what we really care about, or recollecting right now the source of our deepest happiness, or coming back right now to our essential selves. We can explore the terrain of awe, or gratitude, or self-respect, or love. We needn't be fooled by the layers of fear and craving and shame and confusion covering over that light. We can remind ourselves the light is never more than partially covered, and while it may feel remote, it is accessible, always. Because it is always accessible, we are here, now.

It's upon this seed of radiance that we turn toward the good, we nourish it, we cultivate it. It's not up to the nursing staff, or our forebearers, or anybody else. As with the hardy plants I discussed earlier, the latent luminosity within can endure neglect, but it can also thrive when it receives care and attention. Left on its own, the light will survive—half-hidden, quiescent. Nurtured, the light can blaze forth.

5

BEING WITH DIFFICULT
CIRCUMSTANCES

✳

I WAS A SCHEDULED SPEAKER at a gala dinner held to support a non-profit a few years ago. Awaiting my turn to speak, I
was randomly seated at one of the dinner tables. All of us were just
chatting pleasantly when the sponsor of the table leaned over and
said to me, "I hope you're not going to be talking about resilience.
I was already at a resilience luncheon today."

Uh-oh, I thought. Of course, that had been my exact intention,
so in the few minutes left before I was called up to the stage, I

hastily tried to consider, *What else can I possibly call it?* I couldn't really think of an alternative at the last minute, so I had to stick with what I planned, but I felt some sympathy for that woman. It's easy for terms to become clichés, used over and over until they lose their meaning, their ability to stir us into taking action or lead us to new and different ways of thinking.

When we talk about resilience in the face of the difficult circumstances of life, it's usually defined as bouncing back. It's the return after having been lost, resettling after upheaval, repair after disruption. But we're not exactly returning to a status quo that has been frozen, suspended in time, just waiting for us to get back. Life is more dynamic than that. We've been changed by our journey in the dark. The places we're returning to—the people, the relationships, the hopes, the dreams—are ever-changing as well. Life itself is change, and to imagine anything completely static, something we can hold on to absolutely, is to imagine that thing as fixed and cold and immobile—lifeless.

Resilience is also more than being able to maintain what we cling to for security, as environmental scientist Dekila Chungyalpa points out. Dekila is Sikkimese and has been working with Tibetan Buddhist monasteries and nunneries on environmental and climate projects since 2008. She is the founder and director of the Loka Initiative at the University of Wisconsin–Madison, a capacity-building program for faith and Indigenous leaders on environmental and climate issues. She tells us:

> I've spent twelve years doing disaster preparedness with faith leaders.
> And what used to happen was that my way of dealing with my own anxiety around disasters—because we lived in California in a very disaster-prone area for a long

time—was to fill a bugout bag, which is the bag you grab if an earthquake hits. You have all your things in it that you want to take away with you. It's Disaster Preparedness 101.

Every time I'd come home from doing this training, I would sit with my bugout bag and prepare it. It became this exercise of dealing with my own anxiety and dealing with developing resilience, and then lo and behold, an earthquake happened—and I couldn't lift the bag!

It turned out that I filled this bag that was so heavy, so literally filled with my attachments, that it wasn't actually useful. And it was such a wake-up moment for me about what resilience means, because actual resilience is the momentum we create in our minds and in our hearts and in our communities. That's about it.

It is because of the dynamic nature of resilience that we can glimpse the possibility of emerging from a truly difficult situation stronger, or more compassionate, or braver than we were before. It's irrefutable that life contains frustrations, tragedies, disappointments, hurts, and uncertainty. The questions become, "How am I relating to this truth? Is there space for love here?"

This isn't the same thing as *spiritual bypassing*, a phrase coined by psychologist John Welwood to describe using spiritual ideas and practices to dismiss or avoid having to deal with unresolved emotions or difficult psychological issues. That would be more like, "All things are illusory, therefore no need to acknowledge this sadness."

It also isn't the same as *brightsiding*, deflecting from our needs or trying to distance ourselves from reality with platitudes. That's more like speaking to ourselves in the way we sometimes speak to others when trying to be helpful but instead counseling avoidance, which never works long term: "You'll feel better soon . . . There's a lesson here for you to learn . . . This will make you stronger." All of these could very well be true, but maybe not so fast. To follow that counsel as a means to avoid recognizing the pain of a situation is to take our suffering and wrap it up in an opaque layer of denial, hoping to deaden it. The pain, though, pulses with the beat of our own life force, and while it may grow faint and muffled when covered over, in time, it will beckon us. It will call out to us and remind us that it's there. That's why disavowing suffering ultimately doesn't work.

The cognitive psychologist Scott Barry Kaufman, author most recently of *Choose Growth: A Workbook for Transcending*, and whom I discussed in the first chapter, wrote this in *The Atlantic* in August 2021:

> Refusing to look at life's darkness and avoiding uncomfortable experiences can be detrimental to mental health. This "toxic positivity" is ultimately a denial of reality. . . .
>
> The antidote to toxic positivity is "tragic optimism," a phrase coined by the existential-humanistic psychologist and Holocaust survivor Viktor Frankl. Tragic optimism involves the search for meaning amid the inevitable tragedies of human existence, something far more practical and realistic during these trying times.

It reminds me of the rather droll observation of poet Wendell Berry: "Be joyful / though you have considered all the facts."

※

An intriguing aspect of the Buddha's teaching is the understanding that suffering on its own is not inevitably redemptive. We observe this regularly in daily life: we might meet adversity and become bitter and blaming, or we might find that we deepen compassion for ourselves and one another. We might become increasingly self-absorbed, or we might experience ourselves to be part of a larger community of life, and become more connected and caring. We can shut down, enshrouding ourselves in the filaments of our pain or our insistent denial, or we might cultivate interest in the life around us. We might completely identify with a grievous loss or also be in touch with the love that lies at its core, the love that doesn't die.

Expansion and spiritual development and growth can also occur following delightful, uplifting, supportive events. If someone asked me, "Which would you prefer: enhanced spiritual development born from a frightening crisis or born from an inspiring, blissful encounter with someone?" I'd raise my hand right away and say, "I'll take the blissful option, please." But somehow, no one gives us a menu. There is a possibility of emerging from hard times with a bigger heart, a more extensive sense of connection, and an expanded view of life and belonging. It's a real possibility, not just fluff or grandstanding.

The opposite extreme of being in denial, equally unhelpful, is being utterly defined by the painful situation, constricted by it, not seeing any options for relating at all differently, not recognizing any picture of life that is bigger than our circumstance. That bigger picture is the realm those platitudes are trying to usher us toward. But the genuine transformation is discovering we can expand and grow and learn without denying or belittling our difficulties. We start by opening to the pain.

Then we recognize that a primary ingredient in a transformed relationship to painful experience is to have enough light to surround the darkness, an openness big enough to hold the pain and not collapse into it. This is why we practice deepening curiosity, gratitude, kindness, and connecting to others and to a bigger picture of life. That light is genuine light, the potential of the human mind and heart to expand, to see our shared humanity, to be generous without getting depleted, to love no matter what. This possibility is not a test, which we succeed at or fail at—we're not grading ourselves, or comparing ourselves unfavorably to others, or assuming defeat from the first setback. This is an exhortation of what can be possible for us, a step-by-step opening in a lifetime that often deals out challenge, adversity, and distress. It is an assertion of the power of the human spirit, which remains intact within us whatever ordeal we may go through on any given day. It is the portrayal of resilience, renewal, recovery. It is my own heartfelt reflection on what it means to be more fully alive.

As Sojourner Truth said, "Life is a hard battle anyway. If we laugh and sing a little as we fight the good fight of freedom, it makes it all go easier. I will not allow my life's light to be determined by the darkness around me."

How do we make Sojourner Truth's wisdom come alive?

- Remember Viktor Frankl's exhortation to realize tragic optimism rather than indulge in toxic positivity.

- Remember in a previous chapter, handshaking practice and RAIN are possibilities, instead of being confined by corrosive shame or self-blame.

- Explore a regular practice of lovingkindness meditation, and see what changes in presence, openness, and kindness toward yourself and others it might engender in your everyday life.

- Practice habits and ways of relating and forays into new emotional territory. Sometimes we wisely respond to painful circumstances intuitively, not cluttering the space in our minds with fruitless resentment or self-blame. Sometimes we simply remember to breathe because we've been somewhere like this before. At times, the remembrance comes from our family or culture, things we've learned about the power of love or connecting to others along the way. Other times, it feels like we reach right on the spot for skills we've merely heard about because we need something. Nevertheless, those skills can help us move from constriction to flourishing.

With more fully opening to the truth of what is painful as a launchpad, and a vision of all that we are capable of as a North Star, we can learn to breathe more freely, to connect to one another, to live, and to love, even in difficult circumstances. We develop a ministry of presence for ourselves and for the world—a council of connection, tenderness, and caring in the face of both great happiness and inescapable sorrow. And when (not even if) we falter, we can forgive ourselves and begin again. This vision of possibility is realized step by step. As mindfulness teacher Shelly Tygielski, whom we will learn more about later, says, "I will try to, if only for today." Sometimes that effort is halting, sometimes we are stuck for a while, sometimes we fall down altogether. Sometimes "if only for today" feels like a breeze; sometimes it feels like the absolute maximum we can picture. That's real, and that's all right. This kind of vision need not be held as an overidealized image of how we should be, and certainly not as an overidealized image we use as a cudgel to punish ourselves. Sometimes the truth is that the most we can do is ride out a painful situation and try to remember that the truth is that we're not alone.

ILLNESS, PHYSICAL PAIN

PHYSICAL PAIN and illness are both very challenging conditions. I would never want to be glib about the depth of that challenge. Pain and illness both can function like a magnet, drawing in our life force, our hopes, our dreams, our self-confidence, our delight in life—holding these tightly, stifling our vitality, and sundering our connection to the larger world. Yet here, too, even as we're being lured into a frame of mind of completely closing down, there is territory to explore, so we might move from contraction to greater expansion. It's worth investigating, for example, what's occurring when a part of us is in pain and we tighten up the whole rest of our bodies, as though to somehow expel the pain—thereby adding a lot of stress and contraction to what was already painful. We do that on lots of levels. We need to look at that.

Consider, for example, the difference between using language that defines our condition as *who we are* and language that expresses our condition within the larger context of our being. The difference between "I experience epileptic seizures" and "I am an epileptic." When I was a child, we used to laugh at television shows that described the patient in bed number three as "the gallbladder in bed number three," but how do we describe ourselves in our own minds? Only in terms of what is ailing, or also in terms of what is all right? If it is giving us trouble, we could assume that all we are is a giant gallbladder, which makes for an amusing, cartoonish self-portrait (just picture it), but doesn't lead to much creativity or determination or delight in life.

When I was a child, I grew up in a household where a word like *cancer* was whispered, never said out loud with any volume or force. It was evidently a shameful secret, something to be disclosed sparingly and only if necessary. This became crystal clear to me years later, when I was teaching meditation for doctors at an oncology ward at a university hospital, and I experienced the temptation to drop my voice to say the word. It was so weird I had to bring it up, and an interesting discussion ensued about the shame so many feel at a diagnosis, or disability, or injury.

Bob Thurman, a Tibetan Buddhist scholar and author, once said to me, "You should never be ashamed of the suffering you've been through." Bob was passing along a message he'd received many years earlier, after he lost his left eye in an accident. His teacher at the time, a Mongolian monk named Geshe Wangyal, had told him, "Never be ashamed of what happened to you. You have lost one eye but gained a thousand eyes of wisdom."

Acknowledging that wisdom can emerge from pain does not mock the pain itself. It's affirming that we can look at any experience from the fullness of our being and that we can get past the shame and self-denigration we carry. Bob still lost an eye. But if we use our experiences to care for and love ourselves more, and if we use them to connect more deeply with others, then losing an eye can indeed potentially lead to a thousand eyes of wisdom.

Bonnie Pitman is a nationally recognized leader in the museum community, with a career spanning fifty years of service in the museum education and university fields. Since 2008, she has been living with a chronic illness, and in the way she carries herself, she embodies tremendous curiosity and exploration, which I consider gateways to the experience of awe, lifting us from immense and reasonable distress at what we are going through to a fuller picture of what life might have to offer. She told me her inspiring story in a podcast a few years ago:

> I had been healthy most of my life and was off in February of 2008 negotiating a big show for King Tutankhamun. In

Vienna, Austria, I was meeting with the Egyptian delega-
tion, and I felt like I got the flu. I went on to London and
was definitely getting sicker and came home early. When
I came home, everybody, including my doctors, thought,
"Oh, you just have the flu. You're coughing." Finally, when
I couldn't speak anymore and all I could do was cough, I
went to see a specialist who helped me realize what an
unusual condition I was in. I struggled for a number of
years to stay on as the director of the Dallas Museum of
Art, but every time I would go to gatherings or openings,
I would come away sick and go back into the hospital,
because I just couldn't manage being around other people
without picking up their infections.

I was really angry at my body and at myself because my
body was failing me, and I had the job of my dreams. I was
happy doing it. It gave me great fulfillment, but my body
just got weaker and weaker until finally, in 2012, I retired
from the museum. Happily for me, around that time, the
University of Texas hired me, and because teaching was
not as public as being an art museum director, I was able
to succeed and began teaching at the UT Southwestern
Medical School, and also at the Center for BrainHealth
at the University of Texas in Dallas. My life changed.

The illness is still with me today thirteen years later.
It's just a part of who I am, and now I accept it. In the
morning, I do a body scan. . . . After I open my eyes, I
think, "What a gift it is that I'm here and I'm breathing,"
even though every breath hurts almost like a thousand
knives going in and out of my lungs with each breath.
That pain of breathing is a source of life for me. It keeps

me aware, always, of what is present in my life. My choice is not to live in pain. My choice is to live in joy. And so, I think the illness has given me gifts that are way beyond anything I could have ever really understood. I've learned to live with the pain, and I've changed my relationship to it. That's where I am today.

One day in 2011, I woke up from taking a rest, and I wrote down on the pad of paper I keep by my bedside: "I'm going to do something new every day. I'm going to take an ordinary day and make it extraordinary through the power of intention. I can meet new people. I can go to new places. I can have new experiences and do new things with my friend. These experiences could be big or little, and new flavors of ice cream count."

And to this day, there's always ice cream, but it only counts the first time. Last night, I had passion fruit ice cream, which I'd never had.

Life does not have to be the way it was or perfect. Life is never perfect, but it can still be wonderful. My Do Something New practice celebrates the little things in life that can become discoveries and lessons for my life in a larger sense.

Bonnie and I live in different time zones, and as my friends (and often my students if I'm forced to teach too early in the morning) know, I'm a night owl. It might be after midnight my time when I think of Bonnie and check Instagram or Facebook to see what new thing she's gotten up to today. And if she hasn't posted, I go to sleep. I know something will appear the next day, and even if all else has eluded her, it will be a new ice cream flavor.

Bonnie exemplifies what Parker Palmer was pointing to when he said, "It takes no special talent to see what's ugly, numbing, depressing, and death-dealing in our world. But staying aware of what's good, true, and beautiful demands that we open our eyes, minds, and hearts, and keep them open. . . . We can begin to see beauty in the most surprising places, not only in nature but in human nature. That's what will give us the inspiration, strength, and courage to . . . work for what's right. There's a lot of ugly out there, but there's a lot of beauty as well."

COMPASSIONATE SERVICE

I SEE caregivers as the foundation of our society. Many times they are half-hidden, unheralded, yet they are doing the work that makes it all work. Caregiving is a distinctive kind of role in that it literally requires the practice of compassion, opening one's heart, on the job. Caregiving is often a complex endeavor, replete with joys and sorrows, an incredible opening of our hearts coupled with the bitter aftertaste of feeling we are never able to do enough. In some caregiving situations, there is the soul wound of a moral injury, as we wrestle with an intractable health care system that mysteriously doesn't seem to be about care, or are overwhelmed by facing a repeated lack of institutional support for the work we are ceaselessly doing. So often, we find ourselves facing society's casual devaluation of someone we dearly love.

No matter how we try, at times we will be met with challenges: disagreements, pressures, mistakes, moments of forgetfulness, fatigue, anger—the list goes on. I've been leading meditation retreats for caregivers for many years, and I remain moved by the work. Whether they are domestic violence shelter workers, international humanitarian aid workers, first responders, nurses, doctors, hospice workers, therapists, or teachers, their descriptions of the benefits and challenges are striking. So, too, with people caregiving in their personal lives: parents, adult children taking care of their parents, people responding to a partner or spouse stricken by an illness, or people investing in their communities through service to those who are struggling. There is heartbreak, burnout, and lots of fatigue and frustration, yet there is also often a sense of life so much bigger and more sacred than could ever be constrained or compromised by the abilities or health status or neurological condition of the ones we care for.

✳

The Tony Award–winning actor Danny Burstein talked to *Time Out* magazine recently about being hospitalized with COVID and then losing his wife, actress Rebecca Luker, to ALS in late 2020:

> I almost died in the hospital. People were dying around me. My room was right next to the nurses' station, so I could hear what was going on, and I heard people dying, and I heard about the deaths of many people in other rooms near me and in the ICU. And it did change me. And I also, of course, lost my wife, and it made me ... If I learned anything this past year, and I've learned many things, but the most important thing was that you have to live as much as possible and keep going despite all and— and be kind, I'm not kidding. I mean, that's what lasts: being kind and putting goodness and love out there first. That's what matters at the end of the day. Not to be overly dramatic, but watching Becca in the hospital and holding her hand: That's what lasts. All the good things that she put out into the world. The love that you put out into the world,

and the love that I felt for her and she felt for me. That's what lasts. That's why when you have the opportunity to do something for other people that is kind, you should take that opportunity. And when you have the opportunity to do something that you've never done before, that is exciting, do it. I encourage people to live out loud and to live as much as possible.

I have been missing [performing], of course [because of COVID]. But you know, I have a special circumstance because of Becca. If there was a silver lining for me, it's that it gave me time with her that I never, never, never would have had. And I'm grateful for that time because I got to spend all my time with her, taking care of her, and our relationship—as difficult as it may seem—our relationship blossomed in ways that I could have never imagined. We became closer friends and deeper friends, and something beautiful comes about when one person is sick and you discuss things very frankly. I'm grateful for the time I had with her. And it was intense, God knows. But it was also really important and beautiful and filled with love.

NOT IN CONTROL

THERE IS something about just "being with" without trying to assert control over what cannot be controlled that is such a fundamental part of sustainable caregiving. Recognizing our fundamental inability to fix things to suit our personal determination and our timetable, and being able to make ourselves available, present, and loving, is something we can learn to do—and to be okay with.

Acceptance is the energetic opposite of aversion, anger, and fear. It is expansive and warm as opposed to restrictive, imploding, and frozen—all qualities we typically encounter when we fixate on the need to be the savior, to control. This doesn't imply passivity or apathy. We work hard to do all that we can, to seek change or accomplish relief, but it's not a relentless cycle of resistance and resentment fueling our efforts. That just drains away our energy ultimately.

When we're on the front lines of suffering, life itself can start to be viewed as the enemy, too often dealing out betrayal, indifference, or humiliation to someone or several someones we care about. That's why it is so important to remember restoration, resilience—practicing those things that help us move from being locked in constriction, reaction, and feeling deficient to experiencing what is in a more open way.

Mark Coleman, author of *Awake in the Wild,* who teaches meditation, including in nature-oriented retreats, spoke eloquently with me about how restoration is built into all of nature and how we can go with that pattern:

> With any living system, there are times when we engage and are active and times when we need to nourish ourselves. What I learned from Indigenous wisdom in Ecuador was that there is an understanding that between midnight and noon, a tree absorbs nutrients and energy. And from noon to midnight, there's a kind of emitting and radiating. The time to approach a tree is actually from midday to midnight, not when the tree is absorbing and nourishing. This was a beautiful metaphor for me of the fact that the rhythm of life is a flow of giving and receiving. We can't just give, give, give, because we burn out. And we can't just take, take, take, because we become selfish, self-absorbed, and disconnected.

Self-awareness helps us track when it's helpful to be nourishing with whatever resilience-building practices we have. And when it's optimal to give, and serve, and take action. The more we're aware of that balance of giving and receiving, of acting and nourishing, the more resilient we will be for the long haul.

If we don't learn how to nourish, we're going to burn out too soon. It's important for the system that we nourish ourselves and each other, and support each other to do that, as well as take action. It's unrealistic to think anyone can endlessly overlook his or her own needs and still have the energy and commitment to give fully to others. It is essential for those in caregiving roles to cultivate self-compassion alongside compassion for others, to create an inner atmosphere of kindness, expansiveness, and awareness in which resilience can flourish.

Caregiving with resilience first depends on choosing to create a world where we treat ourselves with love, where we know deeply and truly that compassion for ourselves is not weak or self-defeating or an excuse for surrender or passivity. Rather, it is a force that opens the door to a completely different way of relating to others and to our own experience, so we constantly grow and change, and continue to serve.

Dr. Sameet Kumar, a clinical psychologist and Tibetan Buddhist practitioner, has specialized in oncology palliative care for over twenty years and is the author of *Grieving Mindfully: A Compassionate and Spiritual Guide to Coping with Loss*. I asked him once what drew him to working with people who were often deeply suffering, a population many might travel quite a few extra miles to try to avoid. He replied:

> I think what really drew me into work with the dying and the bereaved was my mother. She was born Hindu in what became Pakistan. When the forced partition of the Indian subcontinent occurred in 1947, leading to massive violence, she survived, but her mother, father, and older brother were killed on the train they were using to get to India. She carried those scars with her, and we grew up knowing the deep, traumatic grief she carried inside. She found solace in bhakti yoga [the practice of love and devotion as a path to liberation], and we had a steady stream of sadhus and gurus visiting our home when we lived in India and also after we moved to the U.S. She was a very religious woman, and she raised us not so much to be religious but to be very spiritual. I always grew up with the idea that spiritual practices can hold great pain and they can help the pain be bearable.

In March 2020, when COVID-19 severely hit the southern United States, where Sameet resides, he began taking care of the caregivers. He told me, "Nurses, doctors, respiratory therapists, social workers, medical assistants, chaplains, housekeeping, nutritionists, hospital administration, and my fellow psychologists—everyone was being pulled into the crisis."

It prompted him to offer this counsel for frontline workers, which turns out to be good advice for all of us when we find ourselves in challenging circumstances:

1. **Be kind to yourself.** This is so much bigger than we are. This was something taught to me early on in my training in end-of-life care. You cannot adequately care for others if you are unable to care for yourself. Compassion is not just about how we treat others but also how we treat ourselves. That doesn't mean we have to be perfect. It does mean that we can make choices throughout the day that promote our health and well-being. There is no effort too small to be considered self-care.

2. **Be present.** Every fiber of your being may wish to be somewhere else, doing something else. Be kind to yourself for feeling this way. It's natural. But be present in the moment, even if it is a bad moment.

3. Our automatic urge to flee is **our fight-or-flight response. It takes effort to be present with this stress response and not react.** By becoming aware of our breath and changing how we breathe, we can disrupt this automatic process into one that feels much better and is more present.

4. **Practice diaphragmatic breathing, or belly breathing.** It's a way to be present with and short-circuit the stress response. A technique for belly breathing that I find works is to imagine there's a balloon in your belly. To inhale, inflate the balloon and watch your belly expand. To exhale, deflate the balloon, and watch your belly contract. This is particularly helpful if you count the exhalations, one at a time, so you can keep track of the number of breaths you are taking this way.

5. **You will feel like you are not enough.** It will probably never feel like enough. We fixate on the ones we couldn't

help. We want to have done more, even when we know we couldn't. This is part of compassion, and we have to invite it into ourselves, the same way we care for others. And please, reach out for more help when you need it.

THE JOY AND THE SORROW

I'VE LEARNED that freedom is not about moving away from or transcending all the pain of life in order to travel to an easeful, spacious realm of relief devoid of feeling. We cradle both the immense sorrow and the wondrousness of life at the same time. What does cradling it all mean?

I think of Samantha Novick, whose mother is a teacher at Marjory Stoneman Douglas High School in Parkland, Florida, site of a school shooting in 2018 in which seventeen people were killed. Samantha is quite close to several of the families who lost someone. Samantha recalled the days after the shooting when she "had to find ways to motivate myself to get up and walk out the door." The first time I went to Parkland to lead a meditation workshop, we talked about the quality of equanimity in Buddhist psychology, which doesn't mean indifference or coldness but rather a state that is expansive enough to encompass both the joys of the world and the sorrows of the world, the wondrousness of existence, and the stinging truth that everything in life is so very fleeting.

A state of equanimity is one of space and stillness, as well as connection and compassion. It's an empowered state in which we come to recognize that our capacity for wisdom and love is immense, and these factors never need to be left out of how we are dealing with something.

With her growing mindfulness practice, Samantha recognized

that prior to the shooting she had a "very binary way of thinking about emotions. I could be happy, or I could be sad. I didn't think we could hold more than one emotion at the same time." Samantha now cherishes the Chinese symbol of equanimity: yin and yang. As Samantha put it, "It's easy to get lost in the darkness when it is so relentless. I've learned a lot in holding both. When we are in the depths of darkness, the light is implicit. And when we are in the moments of light, the darkness is implicit and acknowledged. I have also learned from thinking about yin and yang that we can create the light." Now when she's having a tough day, her way out of it is to do something for someone. "Even though I cannot feel the light myself," she said, "I'm going to share it with someone else."

It's that ability to see the yin and yang in any moment that reveals our sense of wholeness. Instead of fixating on avoiding the pain, or being too guilty to take in the joy, we can open our minds and hearts and be in touch with it all. Being that connected to ourselves allows us to feel connected to one another. It returns us to what is intact within us, the capacity for love that we can rely on when so much is disrupted. Amid the chaos of our days, without at all denying the suffering, we can also look for the compassion that does exist in this world. We can look to the people who help and be inspired by their actions. Then, holding that inspiration alongside the honest recognition of suffering, we have the strength and the energy to once more, if only for today, get out of bed, to once more, if only for today, continue to try, and once more, if only for today, leave room for the possibility of interest, connection, resilience, and love in our lives.

As L. R. Knost—founder of the children's rights advocacy and family consulting group Little Hearts / Gentle Parenting Resources—says:

Life is amazing. And then it's awful. And then it's amazing again. And in between the amazing and awful, it's ordinary and mundane and routine. Breathe in the amazing, hold on through the awful, and relax and exhale during the ordinary. That's just living heartbreaking, soul-healing, amazing, awful, ordinary life.

6

HOW WE CAN FEEL MORE EXPANSIVE EVERY DAY

✳

WHEN WE THINK of *awe*, we usually think of encountering something that is vast, that thrills us, that is perhaps beyond our full comprehension. We're rapt, fully present, no part of ourselves left out, no thoughts scattering away to our ordinary distracting preoccupations or litany of complaints. Awe can be reflected in our bodies with goose bumps or chills.

If asked to imagine an awe-inspiring scene, we might immediately think of being out in nature, gazing at a grove of tall redwood or eucalyptus trees (in fact, the scenes of some of the notable research on awe), or looking up in wonder at a sky full of twinkling stars. Our perception of ourselves in relation to the larger world tilts. In this state, people will sometimes say they feel smaller, less significant, or diminished. What I think is diminished, though, is not our sense of inherent worth but our self-preoccupation. We don't feel "less than" or humiliated in any way, because we appreciate ourselves as less separate and more interrelated to the larger existence we're looking at. We're lifted up to it through profound connection. "In experiences of awe, people often speak as if they have found their soul," according to evolutionary psychologist Dacher Keltner, one of the leading researchers on awe and the founding director of the Greater Good Science Center, at the University of California, Berkeley.

Of course, there *are* many occasions we may experience awe with music, with art, with spiritual practice, with one another. I can clearly remember the first time I saw the musical *Hamilton* in a theater on Broadway. It coincided with a time I was working on an earlier book and was feeling pretty discouraged about it. I was late, I wasn't really happy with what I was writing, and I was caught in a tight place of feeling I might not have anything much left to say. "It's your tenth book," ran the defeatist tape in my head. "No one cares what you have to say anymore. Just turn something in."

Just then, a friend came through New York City and offered to take me out to the theater, anything I wanted to see. I chose *Hamilton* because I'd previously turned down a free ticket on three separate occasions to do a good deed each time. This time I made it, quite early in its Broadway run with the original Broadway cast performing. That meant that Lin-Manuel Miranda, who composed the music and wrote the lyrics and the book, was playing Hamilton. I sat there in awe, unable to take my eyes off him, thinking, *You* wrote *this. This all came out of your brain.* And then for myself, *You can never just turn something in, or compromise in that way. Everything you do you have to do with 100 percent of your being.*

My friend still teases me, because at the end of the play when he turned to me and asked if I wanted to go to dinner, he says I got a really strange look on my face and said, "I have to go home and write."

My colleague Joseph Goldstein teases me, too, because he saw *Hamilton* some months after I did. When I asked him how it was, he said, "I really liked it. I didn't have a transcendent experience like you did, but I really liked it."

We may certainly feel awe at different things, in different measures, and at times in circumstances that might be considered by others to be more or less ordinary. Qualities like awe bring us right to the possibility of holding in our hearts the full blessings of life as well as life's fragility and evanescence. Then we put 100 percent of ourselves into everything we do.

Susan Felix, a ceramic artist in Berkeley, California, signs all her correspondence, "Stay amazed." Susan has been a serious ceramic artist for the last fifty years specializing in ritual objects. Her work has been shown at the Museum of Contemporary Crafts in New York City, the Craft and Folk Museum in Los Angeles, and at Christie's in London, UK.

"My work is pit-fired ceramic," she says on her website. "Pit firing, one of the most primitive of firing methods, requires surrender of control over results. I surrender my artwork and control to fire and trust in what will emerge. . . . Just as one day can be more beautiful than the next, I am given differing blessings from the pit."

In other words . . . "stay amazed."

We can't force awe, of course, but we can cultivate the states I've always considered its near cousins: interest and curiosity. If we're distracted, disconnected from what is happening, we're not creating the conditions where awe might arise. If we couldn't care less about what is presenting before us, lost in comparison or reflexive judgment, we're not creating the conditions where awe might arise. How we utilize, frame, and direct our attention is up to us.

In addition to great works of art, majestic forests, or natural grandeur, we can feel awe at people's kindness, at their courage, at their ability to survive through unspeakably challenging conditions. Gregory Boyle, a native Angeleno and Jesuit priest, helped create what would turn into Homeboy Industries, the largest gang intervention, rehab, and reentry program on the planet. His book *Barking to the Choir: The Power of Radical Kinship* shares the wisdom that he's gathered from working closely with "homeboys" for over thirty years. He puts great stock in awe. As he says in his book:

> The ultimate measure of health in any community might well reside in our ability to stand in awe at what folks have to carry rather than in judgment at how they carry it ... Judgment creates the distance that moves us away from each other. Judgment keeps us in the competitive game and is always self-aggrandizing ... Awe is the great leveler. ...
>
> We must try and learn to drop the burden of our own judgments, reconciling that what the mind wants to separate, the heart should bring together. Dropping this enormous inner burden of judgment allows us to make of ourselves what God wants the world to ultimately be: people who stand in awe ... Our practice of awe empties a room, and suddenly there is space for expansive compassion.

Everyday experience—the freedom of a child's laugh, the determination of a student to understand, a gesture of kindness, a glimpse into the fortitude of a parent accompanying their child through suffering and uncertainty—can also move us to awe, and we live in a different way when it does.

It's awe-inspiring in and of itself that our bodies work (or adapt to work differently), that our consciousness is mutable and that change is possible, and that most times we can get up out of bed and have a day.

I first came upon writer, rapper, and storyteller Joél Leon (formerly Joel L. Daniels) on Twitter. After I found myself liking or retweeting every single thing he tweeted, I thought, *This is ridiculous. I should just talk to him,* and that's when I reached out and began inviting him on my podcast. Joél specializes in moderating and leading conversations surrounding race, masculinity, mental health, creativity, and the performing arts, with love at the center of his work and purpose. He says, "We put so much pressure on ourselves to make something extraordinary out of this existence of ours when, in reality, our breath, the mere presence of our flesh, our feet touching the ground and our hands reaching for a forever-burning sun is as extraordinary as we need to be."

> *Cages or wings*
> *Which do you prefer?*
> *Ask the birds*
>
> —JONATHAN LARSEN, FROM THE SONG
> "LOUDER THAN WORDS," IN THE MUSICAL
> *TICK, TICK . . . BOOM!*

In positive psychology, awe is considered in the same realm as states like gratitude, serenity, interest, hope, inspiration, pride (self-respect), and love (lovingkindness). Barbara Fredrickson, a researcher at the University of North Carolina at Chapel Hill who specializes in studying these positive qualities, has developed a theory she calls "broaden and build." According to Fredrickson's theory, positive qualities are not just feel-good states to be enjoyed or indulged in. They are, rather, the basis for a broadened scope of awareness, along with a potent sense of capacities we hold within ourselves.

They allow us to develop our consciousness to include a wider array of thoughts, actions, and perceptions. We can broaden our scope of awareness and become more connected to our own experiences and feelings, as well as those of others. In one of my favorite examples of this phenomenon, at Bob Dylan's induction into the Rock & Roll Hall of Fame in 1988, Bruce Springsteen described hearing Dylan's music for the very first time. Springsteen was fifteen, he said, riding in the car with his mother, idly listening to the radio, when "Like a Rolling Stone" came on. It was as though, Springsteen recalled, "somebody took his boot and kicked open the door to your mind."

His mother's verdict: "That man can't sing." I guess it wasn't quite as positive an experience for his mother!

I love that sense of expansion, of no longer feeling in the grip of the merely conventional or the routine, but glimpsing new possibilities, sensing the chance for movement, not being held in or held back. That door having been kicked in, light we might not have believed in before is allowed in. Previously, we might not have believed in its efficacy or in its existence. The conceptual connections we make expand. We come up with more and better ideas. When we face problems, this broadening of perspective makes our solutions better. Positivity opens us. It allows us to consider possibilities that are otherwise hidden from view.

Apparently, the broadening effect of positive states actually improves our peripheral vision! I keep working to confirm the research in my own experience, because I just find it spooky! (I'm also thinking I have to do something really positive-state-inducing before the visual test for my next driver's exam.) That peripheral vision expansion leads to a deeper felt sense of everything around us.

"Your positivity and your openness feed on and reinforce each other," Fredrickson says, "creating a buoyant upward spiral within you. Positivity also alters how you see your connections with others. You think *we* instead of *me*. With positivity, you see new possibilities, bounce back from setbacks, connect with others, and become the best versions of yourself."

According to Fredrickson, positive emotions also build inner resources, a sense of strength from within we can draw upon for service to others—as well as during trying times for ourselves. Shelly Tygielski, a mindfulness teacher and author of the book *Sit Down to Rise Up*, has often used a phrase I particularly like: "Enough is a feast." If you are terrified, if you feel impoverished within, if you feel perpetually humiliated, enough will never seem like enough. If you are in touch with inner strength, energy, uplift, enough is more than enough—like a feast.

When we feel hollow within, we are pulled to the grasping and craving, mindless consumerism, and aimless competition that so much conventional culture invites us to. But if we can step away from the dictates of the ordinary, we can see reality in a fresh and a more truthful way. We can access inner sufficiency—even abundance—and resourcefulness, a wellspring of energy within that allows us to connect, offer, create. If we are taught to believe we could never *have* enough, we're not motivated to give, to share with others. The threat we imagine is that we will be left with nothing, or left shatteringly bereft, with less than nothing. If we feel lost in the whirlwind of our own unworthiness, if we're taught to believe we could never *be* enough, we don't have nearly the energy to fully care about others. We are not moved to try to offer anything, because we are sure it could never be worthy or impressive or good enough.

Building our inner resources doesn't mean becoming indifferent to the need to seek external change. Not at all. It is the foundation of creative, unforced, heartfelt actions of all kinds. We build inner resources so as not to feel so depleted all the time, with nothing to draw upon in periods of challenge and too tired to fully experience periods of joy.

This doesn't mean we're hell-bent on positivity and ignore the pain we may feel. As gratitude researcher Robert Emmons of the University of California, Davis, wrote in the online *Greater Good* magazine: "To deny that life has its share of disappointments, frustrations, losses, hurts, setbacks, and sadness would be unrealistic and untenable . . . No amount of positive thinking exercises will change this truth."

I once attended a retreat focused on aging led by Tsoknyi Rinpoche, whose handshake practice we saw in chapter 3. Although he was still a fairly young man at that point, Rinpoche had noticed that many of his students were confronting the challenges of growing older. Aging is a mixed bag. Wisdom, perspective, gratitude—so many things grow stronger as we get older. But there are also distressing, growing incapacities from one's body, fear of what a moment of forgetfulness might mean, the sheer indignity of being treated as unimportant by some, the frustration of having to scroll down for a long, long, long time on some websites to get to the year of your birth (my personal pet peeve). And then there is the painful fact, so relevant more recently, that one's body tends not to mount as strong an immune response in relation to vaccines as you get older.

One afternoon, someone in the retreat was waxing on about the tremendous joys and delights of growing older. Exhilarating insights followed a litany of pleasures followed impressive triumphs, all spoken faster and faster (*What is she running from?* I thought darkly) until Rinpoche interrupted her. "Don't just make a poem out of aging," he said. "It can be really hard sometimes."

He wasn't encouraging cynicism or despair—more an invitation to see and openly acknowledge all aspects of our experience. One thing we don't need is to deny the difficult. We also don't need to be completely defined by what is difficult—no breathing space, backed into a corner, more and more overcome by what is already painful and can soon become crushing. Being enveloped in and defined by what's difficult is relatively easy to do. It takes some intentionality to recognize all aspects of our experience and remember the positive forces in our lives.

To grow the positive emotions that help us "broaden and build" is empowering, because from that place of strength and openness, we can see the essential truths of our lives more clearly—the paradoxes, the ambivalence, the layers, the continual element of change. In addition, we have the courage to not try to sweep aside what we do uncover.

In our time—when cynicism is often valued over inspiration and love is seen as simply being naive—any of these expansive qualities we've been considering may seem like the hypocritical option of people-pleasers or dupes. All of these qualities we've been considering—such as gratitude, serenity, interest, hope, lovingkindness—require a much deeper exploration for us to assess their genuine power and/or weakness. In addition, every expansive quality can easily have a shadow side, a distorted form of the state we're seeking to cultivate, one that misleads us and does us no favors on a path to liberation. A genuine exploration of these states is warranted from that angle as well.

We would never want to pretend, or feel coerced into, or directed to assume a quality we are not actually feeling. "Your body knows the difference between real sincere positivity and put-on positivity," says Barbara Fredrickson. What would be the point? We can craft our lives toward true freedom, rather than chasing the display of *seeming* to feel something only to be putting on a show for the sake of others.

In the same *Atlantic* piece quoted in the previous chapter, cognitive psychologist Scott Barry Kaufman discussed the dynamics of "post-traumatic growth," indicating that researchers have found that

> people can grow in many ways from difficult times—including having a greater appreciation of one's life and relationships, as well as increased compassion, altruism, purpose, utilization of personal strengths, spiritual development, and creativity. Importantly, it's not the traumatic event itself that leads to growth ... but rather how the event is processed.

It's that "how the event is processed" that is the central target of our challenge. We work to have the broadest possible perspective and a core of inner strength we can reach toward to help us see our way through.

GRATITUDE

A FRIEND of mine, Linda Stone, whom we met in chapter 1, is a blogger and tech thought leader who coined the phrase *continuous partial attention,* which I find a pretty good description of our normal state of fragmentation. She also coined the phrases *email apnea* and *screen apnea,* which means "a temporary absence or suspension of breathing, or shallow breathing, while doing email or at a screen." Email apnea can contribute to a stress response in the body. This stress response can compromise effective use of our attention and, over time, can contribute to a variety of health issues. Linda, observing me checking my email once, made the sad pronouncement that, indeed, email apnea aptly described my condition. (She was right.)

Linda has long tuned into the ways we use attention. "Attention is the most powerful tool of the human spirit," she says. "We can enhance or augment our attention with practices like meditation, breathwork, and exercise, diffuse it with technologies like email, texting, and social media, or alter it with pharmaceuticals. In the end, though, we are fully responsible for how we choose to use this extraordinary resource." Linda has studied vagal tone, as well as a variety of techniques, including awareness of the breath and conscious breathing, that strengthen embodied attention, work to rebalance the nervous system, and help to regulate emotions. *Vagal tone* is the term used to describe the body's ability to recover from stress. This is important both for our overall health and for effectively using our attention.

One of these breathing techniques is to:

> *inhale* for a count of four,
> *hold* your breath for a count of four, and
> *exhale* for a count of eight.

There are various ways of doing this. The main point is that the exhale should be longer than the inhale. This is a powerful tool for shifting from a cascade of stress reactions to a calmer state. No technique, though, works absolutely all the time or as quickly as we would like. In addition, whatever tool or technique we pick up, it works best when we can infuse it with a sense of appreciation toward ourselves and others. We are relying on that scaffolding as we work toward coming back into balance and feeling some ease of being.

Linda recounted to me her experience of cultivating attention, calm, and vagal tone with the help of HeartMath, which is a technology that aims to improve emotional well-being by helping users to change their heart rhythm pattern to "create physiological coherence; a scientifically measurable state characterized by increased order and harmony in our mind, emotions and body." The HeartMath device measures heart rate variability, an indicator of the flexibility of our response to stressors. Linda told me this story:

> When I was first starting to think about email apnea, at first I tried a few different breathing practices and taking breaks. Then I discovered the HeartMath technology. I would put on a heart rate variability ear clip from a HeartMath device. The display showed three colors: red, green, and blue. Red meant I was not in a good place. Green meant I was headed to a good place. Blue meant I was in a good place.
>
> During the time I was experimenting with this, I had a chance to visit HeartMath and meet with Rollin McCraty, the HeartMath Institute's research director. We talked about breathing techniques that would be helpful for managing my heart rate variability throughout the day. I was having mixed success with the breathing techniques I was using.
>
> He looked at me and said, "Feelings of love, gratitude, and appreciation can get you there almost immediately."

I had been so fixated on email apnea being about temporary cessation of breath and shallow breathing that I found it hard to believe that focusing on emotions like love and gratitude could be more effective than employing a breathing technique.

Not long after that, I was giving a talk to a gathering of about forty tech people, and I began to demonstrate using the HeartMath device to help with awareness and management of email apnea. I was explaining one of the most popular breathing techniques for managing vagal tone and relaxing the body: the breathing technique where the exhale is twice as long as the inhale. I was demonstrating it, and nothing was changing: red, red, red, red. Presenting in front of a crowd had me feeling so stressed that I wasn't able to perform. I had not yet tried what Dr. McCraty had suggested, but I decided to go for it! "The other way to do this is to feel a sense of embodied love, appreciation, or gratitude." I looked out at the people, many of whom I'd been acquainted with for many years, and I said, "I'm going to look over at Matt, who I'm very grateful to for helping me shift to a better blogging technology." Just as I started to look at Matt and to say this, I heard people gasp, "You're there!" Once I felt the sense of embodied gratitude, it took only seconds to shift away from the stress response. For me, that was a powerful realization as to how emotion is at the heart of real life. Emotions like love and appreciation, especially when we can experience them not just mentally but more fully, in an embodied way, can help antidote the stress from email apnea, as well as other daily stressors.

David DeSteno, professor of psychology at Northeastern, would support this understanding of embodied appreciation, or gratitude. His recent papers include "Gratitude Reduces Consumption of Depleting Resources" and "The Grateful Don't Cheat: Gratitude as a Fount of Virtue," and in 2021, he published *How God Works: The Science Behind the Benefits of Religion*. On YouTube, you can also watch a talk he gave at Google in 2018, "Emotional Success: The Power of Gratitude." His research suggests that with increased gratitude, people tend to become more generous, more willing to help others, more reluctant to cheat, and more willing to share profits. He paints a picture of someone who is less impulsive, more cooperative, suffering less from stress, and less ruled by materialism.

"Gratitude gives us more patience," DeSteno says. "It focuses us on long-term gains over short-term satisfaction." In a podcast discussion with me, he elaborated on his understanding of gratitude's power and why it's not about turning us into suckers or doormats:

> Every emotion we have exists for the future, not for the past. It doesn't make sense for the brain to waste its metabolic energy having you feel stuff if you can't change anything about it. The reason I feel gratitude, and I feel grateful to you, is because it motivates us to then repay those favors in the future to the person who helped us, our benefactor, or to pay it forward to other people.

It's helpful to conduct our own personal experiment around gratitude reflections, to discover if in fact we are left more credulous or passive or are actually emboldened by them. Scott Barry Kaufman has said, "In recent years, scientists have begun to recognize that the practice of gratitude can be a key driver of post-traumatic growth after an adverse event, and that gratitude can be a healing force. Indeed, a number of positive mental-health outcomes are linked to a regular gratitude practice, such as reduced lifetime risk for depression, anxiety, and substance-abuse disorders."

Could a recommendation of practicing gratitude be used by a manipulative system to try to induce docility and a kind of stupefied satisfaction? I think certainly yes. But wouldn't it be especially fulfilling, then, to use that very practice to fuel the inner resources we need to seek change in the system?

The Reverend Cathy Bristow offers an especially powerful gratitude reflection, which she demonstrated on a podcast with me. Reverend Cathy is an ordained interfaith minister and the founder and principal of Bridges, a consulting firm whose mission is to re-language and initiate fresh conversations about race, gender, and diversity. She is deeply involved in social justice work and provides free seminars on brain health and the impact of spirituality. One of her main focuses is to mentor women dealing with the effects of systemic racism, subjugation, and prejudice to help them transform despair into healing capacities for compassion, forgiveness, innovation, and creativity.

REFLECTION ON THE GOOD

Allow yourself to think about this day, something that's happened that's good. It doesn't have to be a magnificent thing. Maybe it's simply a meal. Perhaps someone smiled on the subway. Maybe someone let you get in line first. Maybe you saw a baby playing.

Something good. Go through your day; go through the time that's passed. The day, a couple of hours, what happened that's good?

When you find those, connect to the feeling that happened, for just a moment that good-tasting meal might've made you smile. The flower growing where you didn't think it would grow might've given you an instant of wonder and awe. That baby laughing might've reminded you that life is continuing as it should in ways we don't know. Allow yourself to connect those feelings and bring back those feelings of the good things. It's called gratitude, gratitude.

And if it works for you, say thank you. Thank you, little miracles. Thank you, little good things. Thank you, little moments of smiling, little instances of joy, little times of happiness. Say thank you. And then take those experiences of gratitude and allow yourself to breathe them in, the gratefulness, the gratitude.

Know that as we practice looking for the good moments, looking for what to be grateful for, it becomes a habit. We see what we're looking for. We shift our moods. We're more in our lives at that moment. We're living large.

YES, AND . . .

SOMETIMES "PRACTICING GRATITUDE" can feel like bulldozing over your feelings—especially when you're not starting out feeling particularly grateful at all. Whenever we feel like we *should* be grateful or *must* be grateful, that's a bad sign. It means that we're dividing our experience into what we're presenting publicly and the feelings we're hiding within, and it's an awkward and painful way of dealing with ambivalence.

"Yes, and . . ." thinking—as it's known in improv theater—is one more skillful way of sitting in the center of paradox or ambivalence, being there to take it all in, and relating skillfully to whatever presents itself.

In improvisation, it looks like this: No matter what gets presented onstage, instead of negating it, disparaging it, or disagreeing with it, your job is to accept the scenario as it's presented to you and then add to it. Otherwise, the conversation or piece just stops in its tracks.

"Yes, and . . ." doesn't mean you agree with what's just been said or like it, but you're going to acknowledge it and build from there, rather than getting stuck in fighting what has come before. In business or family settings, it's a tool that can strengthen communication, facilitate brainstorming, and open up more creative spaces.

In gratitude practice, it might look like this: Reflecting on December holidays and the angst that often comes from visiting relatives, Pooja Lakshmin, M.D., suggested in *The New York Times* that our usual way of thinking, "Why do I put in all of this time and effort every year? I got to see Grandma, *but* everyone else was terrible," be reframed as "I got to spend time with my grandmother in a way that was low risk *and* everyone else was terrible." Both can be true. We can acknowledge the presence of distressing or antagonistic or mean-spirited family members *and* also be so incredibly grateful for the chance to hug and chuckle with and speak softly to Grandma.

PRIDE

PRIDE IS a difficult word to understand in this context. When we use the word *pride* conventionally, it often refers to conceit or arrogance, evoking the specter of the seven deadly sins and the taint of vainglory. We say pride makes people's heads swell or that pride comes before a fall. That kind of pride becomes hubris. Pride as a *positive state* actually means self-respect.

Many of us have been taught that we will find self-respect by denigrating others. Our worlds become based on continual comparison, scanning for others' faults, resentful of others' happiness. In contrast, true self-respect fosters a power of generosity, so we don't feel diminished by the joy of others. What a relief that is!

We also quite often fall into the habit of self-denigration. In my years of teaching meditation, countless times someone will begin a question with, "I know this is a stupid question, but . . ." That first phrase reveals a lot—why don't we believe we have the right to ask a question, to take up some space, seek greater understanding of something? There really are no stupid questions, full stop.

Self-respect is caring for oneself without the drag of self-preoccupation. Imagine a world in which you treated yourself as well as you treat your closest friends, family, and other loved ones. Self-respect can come from reflecting on the goodness that moves through us, the goodness we are capable of, the goodness we're bringing to the collective. Conceit will cause us to be stuck in a fixed view of who we are. Self-respect can lead to expansive thinking, a greater belief in our capabilities, and taking action.

Pride, in the positive sense, is what emerges within that causes us to hold our heads up and breathe easy after an accomplishment, when we've invested our time, our hearts, our energy. In the last little while, I've had friends extol the good feeling they got when they finally ran that marathon, finished a poem they started twenty years before, apologized and cleared the slate with someone, thanked someone long overdue, put out their thoughts about a controversy, planted a garden, and recognized they made a difference to someone through mentoring.

Sometimes it's not an achievement that generates pride as much as including ourselves within a circle of possibility by not withdrawing to the sidelines or denigrating our capacity to grow or change. Research shows that when people feel pride, they are more likely to persist on difficult tasks. And the mindscape of pride is expansive. It kindles dreams of further achievements: "If I can do this, maybe I can . . ."

In 1979, His Holiness the Dalai Lama made a visit to Massachusetts and came to the Insight Meditation Society in Barre. We had a retreat going on at the time, and after the Dalai Lama addressed the meditators, there was time for questions. One young man (who had been meditating for about two weeks at that point) said, "I feel very discouraged. I don't think I have any capacity for developing insight or compassion."

The Dalai Lama looked a little surprised and responded, "That's just wrong." And went on to explain the potential that exists inside every person for growth and change. Potential that doesn't have to be duly earned; it just is.

It's funny, because several people complained to me afterward, saying that it is bad pedagogy to tell someone they're wrong. Yet as the retreat went on for several weeks and we kept working together, it became clear that it was a very important message for the young man. It was a very important message for me as well. I think of that conversation sometimes when I meet someone who is assuming definite defeat before they even start something: "I can't do anything worthwhile." I think about it when I get discouraged and could imagine taking it deeply to heart, forgetting for a bit that discouragement is a set of thoughts and feelings that can be looked at mindfully like any other thoughts or feelings. And I think about it when I doomscroll through news of the world and think, *Well, there's clearly no difference at all I could ever make, either to one person or to the larger community.* Then I remind myself of the Dalai Lama in the meditation hall at IMS and think, *Let's see if "that's just wrong" still holds.* So far . . . it's still at 100 percent true.

One technique that Barbara Fredrickson encourages for cultivating self-respect is building a pride portfolio. To start on your pride portfolio, consider:

When have you felt proudest of yourself, most fully confident in your abilities, and most self-assured?

When have you done something praiseworthy? Achieved something through your own concerted efforts?

What makes you hold your head high and stand up tall?

What makes you want to share your good news with others?

What draws you to dream big, into visions of what you might accomplish in the future?

A MORAL COMPASS

A CLASSICAL PATH to intensifying one's self-respect is through the practice of morality—not being moralistic, which would tend toward confinement, repression, judgment of oneself, and even persecution of others, but rather basing our lives on a vision of compassionate non-harming that strengthens our moral sensitivity. Our lives get bigger, more open, when we have a moral center, because we have built a foundation for greater empathy and, therefore, intimacy with all of life. When we dedicate ourselves to actions that do not hurt ourselves or others, our lives become all of one piece, a "seamless garment" with nothing separate or disconnected.

When we live with integrity, we also further enhance confidence in ourselves by being able to rejoice, taking active delight in our actions. Rejoicing opens us tremendously, brightening our vitality, our gratitude, and our love.

Many of us find moral or ethical reflection embarrassing. So often we're taught to put the emphasis on all the unfortunate things we've done, all the disturbing mistakes we've made. These shouldn't be overlooked, but those actions do not reflect all of who we are or what we're capable of. However, this classical reflection is also not a way of increasing conceit, by basking in our moral superiority. It is rather a commitment to our own caring for ourselves, seeing that as the basis for a caring closeness with *all of life*. It fills us with joy and love for ourselves and a great deal of self-respect.

We can reflect on the good things we have done, recollecting times when we have been generous or times we have been caring. Perhaps we can think of a time when it would have been easy to hurt somebody, or to tell a lie, or to be dismissive, yet we made the effort not to do that. Perhaps we can think of a time when we gave something up in a way that freed our mind and helped someone else. Or perhaps we can think of a time when we have overcome some fear and reached out to someone. These reflections open us to a wellspring of happiness that may have been hidden from us before, a happiness that brings us closer to others and reshapes our lives.

✳

What happens to our pride, our self-respect, if we fall down, if we don't live up to the vision we've had about ourselves? It seems that as we grow into our personal and professional identities, we often begin to view ourselves as static entities:

"I do *this* for a living. *This* is who I am."

"I'm a fearful person and I always will be."

"I failed to live up to my ideals; therefore, I am a failure."

In fact, we are processes, dynamic systems constantly in flux. And as dynamic systems, we are naturally creative—we have the ability to reinvent through disruption and the capacity for reorganization and self-repair when we've been physically or emotionally challenged.

We can remember (as in rejoin with) our deeper values, fundamental commitments, helpful ways of being that might have eroded or been flung away. Any system loses creativity by getting stuck in fixedness or rigidity, by losing its flexibility.

What does this mean day to day? We fall down, and we can pick ourselves up or let someone help us up, and we start over. We are moving along a certain track and we realize it's the wrong direction, and we need a course correction. We make a mistake, we take an honest look at it for lessons learned or for a way to make amends, and we begin again. Recognizing our potential to make amends, to start over, to try can all be sources of self-respect.

In this way, pride broadens our mindsets by reminding us about different and kinder ways we want to live. We can respect the ways we've tried to make a difference and be energized to move closer to an integrated life.

7

WE ARE NOT ALONE

✳

CONNECTION IS a profound human need. Perhaps because I know so many people who spend vast amounts of time alone and also are flourishing, I like the distinction between *solitude* and *loneliness*. Loneliness has elements of feeling abandoned, discounted, not belonging. It's an incredibly painful, constricted state. In Tibetan Buddhism, the term for the intermediate state between death and rebirth is known as the *bardo*. It is said that at first in the bardo, you may not even realize you've died. As Bob Thurman said to me once, "Maybe you're at dinner and you can't figure out why nobody seems to be passing you the butter."

Loneliness can be a kind of bardo, a place where we feel we've been erased. We are stranded in some adjunct world, unacknowledged, disconnected. An extra-poignant element is how lonely we might feel even waking up next to an intimate partner, or within a family structure. We can feel lonely and emotionally abandoned even when we're surrounded by other people. What defines loneliness is our internal degree of discomfort: we yearn for things to be other than the way they are.

Solitude, by contrast, is a state where we may be alone in terms of actual contact with others, but we have ease of heart. Many of us undertake solitude as a chance to connect with ourselves without distraction or disturbance. It can enhance our personal growth and resilience.

Loneliness is a much tougher thing to feel. There are varied reasons we have seen a surge in loneliness. Participation in many social and civic structures that used to bring people together— bowling leagues, clubs, professional associations, guilds—has declined; close alliances with institutions like churches or synagogues have waned for some people. We live in a more atomized society. An outsized emphasis on individualism is often coupled with a worldview of scarcity, a pervasive need to accumulate as much as I can for me and mine. No time to stop and smell the roses, let alone chat with a neighbor. Overreliance on technology, too, can play a role. (Ironically, since it promises great connection yet so often leads to immense isolation.)

I remember a woman in New York City saying to me some years ago that what she missed the most were the random conversations she might have with someone sitting next to her on a bus or waiting in line at the grocery store, or sitting on the stoop of her building with a little-known neighbor. "Now," she said, "everyone's face is buried in their phones. No one talks anymore."

Isolated though we are, we count on little moments of reinforcement: Yes, we belong. . . . Yes, we are a part of things. . . . Yes, someone in fact hears us as we ask for the butter.

Barbara Fredrickson, Ph.D., whom we met in the previous chapter, found in her research that moments of what she calls *microconnection* (laughing with someone at a shared sight, exchanging surprised observations, hugging someone, smiling at a stranger's dog on the street) actually strengthen the functioning of our vagus nerve, the longest cranial nerve that stretches through the abdomen, and helps us deal more skillfully with the fight-or-flight stress response and protects the body against stress-induced inflammation. Friendliness, connection, lovingkindness, compassion—and variations thereof—are as supportive as can be.

COVID of course made things much worse. Not everyone was physically isolated, but many were. I remember doing a Zoom webinar, and someone wrote in the chat, "I live in a nursing home. I haven't had a visitor in a year," which I found just heartbreaking. Friends have told me about standing out in snowbanks to talk to their elderly parent through a window. And those working every day outside the home, with more physical contact, or living in multigenerational households might not have been gathering in the larger faith-based or social groups they were accustomed to go to for renewal.

COVID, too, provided us with new opportunities to find one another, and to care for one another. I remember people in New York telling me things like, "I've lived in this building for twelve years. I never even knew the names of my neighbors. Now we all have one another's phone numbers so we can check in with each other."

Rev. Cathy Bristow, whose gratitude reflection we saw in the previous chapter, brought this kind of effort to a wider group in her not-alone project, a twenty-four-hour free phone-in service for medical professionals staffed with volunteer chaplains, therapists, and healers offering contemplative practices of deep listening, prayer, meditation, and breathing exercises. She met the suffering of the pandemic with love. As she recounted to me:

> Like so many people during the pandemic, I became so constricted. I thought, *What can I do? I can't do anything. I'm here in the house. I've got to wear my mask. I can't.* I had lots of can'ts, lots of prohibitions, lots of don't-do-thats. And then I thought, *Well, wait a minute, wait a minute. I can do something.*
>
> I rented an 800 line, and individuals agreed to volunteer for hours during the twenty-four-hour day to be available for only five minutes with callers. With volunteers spread across time zones, we could cover the clock. As volunteers, we gathered and shared contemplative practices, rituals. Then, for the callers, we had a standard format. When you answer the phone, you say, "I'm here for you. Now we have five minutes on the phone and we can do one of these things. I can listen to whatever it is you want to tell me. We can pray. We can meditate, or we can be silent and just do breathing exercises here together." A few of our volunteers would even sing, if people wanted that. And then just before the time is over, you say, "We're almost at the end, how would you like to close out?"
>
> We used that fixed time of five minutes because hospitals agreed to allow the 800 number to be posted and used not as part of a break time or you've-got-to-ask-your-

supervisor time. You could go access it right then and there, when you walk away from your workstation briefly or go to the bathroom.

It was a privilege for all of us who listened to hear people and to stand with them and represent love in a way that just says, "I'm present. I am your human connection for this short time, someone who cares that you are caring for all of us." What a powerful statement to say to another human being. To create circles of caring, to create community and connectivity, we might need to step out of our comfort zones and do things a little differently, connecting with people whom we have not considered connecting with and being vulnerable with before.

I am so delighted at the thought of someone singing to me for five minutes . . . maybe a lullaby when I can hardly admit how tired I am, or a marching song when I need some get-up-and-go!

Connection is our greatest source of expansiveness. Ultimately, connection is an inner state. I know introverts who would never dream of striking up a conversation with a stranger. I don't think that consigns one to loneliness. There is something about feeling we have presented ourselves authentically that belies loneliness. We want to be validated for who we are, but how we are seen is something we cannot actually control, even in intimate relationships. We probably all know people who tend to be surrounded by others or have a life partner who seem to be the loneliest of all. In the end, the foundation of our feeling connected instead of fragmented or split off is being in touch with the fullness of our own being and bringing that into how we relate.

Even as I would read studies about the powerful healing force of social connection in various clinical conditions, I would reflect that it can't always be reduced to a numbers game, like, "I only have three friends; I need six." That can be an important thing to contemplate at times, and I've seen people work to repair relationships that had foundered or get creative about crafting new relationships when faced with how isolated they had become. I also believe there is an inner, rock-bottom sense of connection that is the most essential thing of all.

I have a friend who was hospitalized with COVID in 2021. He was steadily getting better, appreciating the medical care, and feeling lucky to have his own room. Then suddenly, as he was nearing discharge, he was given a roommate, also diagnosed with COVID. The man was admitted at night, with a curtain drawn partitioning the room, so my friend couldn't see him, but he could hear him. Resentful at being given a roommate, and mostly frightened that he might get sick again in proximity to the new patient, he couldn't sleep for hours. Finally, he decided to do lovingkindness meditation (a form of offering blessings or good wishes), silently repeating phrases for his roommate: "May you be happy; may you again be healthy; may you have a peaceful heart." For hours.

Finally, comforted by the sense of connection, he fell asleep. When he first encountered the man the next day, he was startled to hear, "There's such a calm, lovely energy coming from your side of the room. It helped me a lot." We get a glimpse sometimes of layers and layers of connection, delicate, immeasurable, because that's the deeper truth of things. However alone or cut off we might feel, this world in truth is one of interdependence, of relatedness.

WEB OF LIFE

THINKING OF that deep connectedness reminds me of Suzanne Simard, professor of forest ecology at the University of British

Columbia, who discovered that trees are involved in a constant exchange of resources and information via underground fungal networks. In a series of experiments, she learned that trees are connected to one another through vast and complex underground fungal root systems known as *mycorrhizal networks,* or quite amusingly dubbed the Wood Wide Web.

Via this subterranean pipeline, trees connect with other trees. Simard explains that we can think of nodes in a network as being like individual computers, and the network as the space the information moves through. Hubs, like Google, are places where lots of nodes gather together and vast amounts of information are shared.

In the Wood Wide Web, each individual tree is a node, while older trees, often larger and taller, are hubs, where lots of information and connection happen. Mycelia, a network of fungal threads, is the connective tissue linking all the nodes, the hubs, and all vegetation—creating a web. By tightly wrapping itself closely to the roots of the hub tree, the mycelia creates a pathway for water, nutrients, and other chemicals to travel between the cells of the roots and the mycelia.

Since hub trees tend to tower over the others, they have more exposure to sunlight. This can result in the hub tree producing more sugar than it needs through photosynthesis. Once it has used what sugar it needs to sustain itself, the rest is generously shared through the mycelium network to support other trees.

Water is another resource a hub tree can share. By sharing water and other nutrients, the hub supports its seedlings' growth and the growth of other trees. The sharing goes both ways: if at some point the hub tree is stressed and needs resources, the mycelia and other trees send water and nutrients back to the hub.

In addition to sharing resources, the Wood Wide Web is used to send out warnings. For example, if a tree is attacked by a bark beetle, it can send out a warning signal, known as a *defense signal.* When the other trees receive the defense warning through the mycelia, they're able to increase their defenses and more effectively ward off attacks.

As Simard so beautifully expresses in *Finding the Mother Tree:*

> **On Interconnectedness:** The trees soon revealed startling secrets. I discovered that they are in a web of interdependence, linked by a system of underground channels, where they perceive and connect and relate with an ancient intricacy and wisdom that can no longer be denied. I conducted hundreds of experiments, with one discovery leading to the next, and through this quest I uncovered the lessons of tree-to-tree communication, of the relationships that create a forest society.
>
> **On Wisdom:** The old trees nurture the young ones and provide them food and water just as we do with our own children. It is enough to make one pause, take a deep breath, and contemplate the social nature of the forest and how this is critical for evolution. The fungal network appears to wire the trees for fitness. And more. These old trees are mothering their children.
>
> *The Mother Trees.*
>
> When Mother Trees—the majestic hubs at the center of forest communication, protection, and sentience—die, they pass their wisdom to their kin, generation after generation, sharing the knowledge of what helps and what harms, who is friend or foe, and how to adapt and survive in an ever-changing landscape.

That portrayal—of connection, of fulfilling our destiny by caring for one another, of offering nourishment to those in need and assuming the mantle of legacy toward those yet to come—is a vision of life that lifts us and opens our hearts to whatever we may be going through.

Seeing the backdrop of the cover of this book reminded me of one of the most brilliant and best-known images in the teachings of Buddhism: Indra's net. In Indra's net, the universe is described as a net of infinite proportions. At each interlacing point, where the strings of the net meet, there is a multifaceted, highly reflective jewel, like a diamond or a piece of crystal. Each jewel reflects the others, including the reflected images held in the others.

To look at one jewel, at one point, is to see the reflection of all jewels, at all points. To look at ourselves is to discover all beings and all things in the universe; to look at others is to see ourselves as well. Every event, every entity, every emotion, every experience we have is born out of a web of interconnectedness. In all of existence, there is no one and no thing that stands apart.

In day-to-day life, this translates into a much more realistic perception of the larger patterns and confluences we are all actually a part of. You might reflect: Who are you counting on? Who is counting on you? How many people, how many relationships, how many joys, how many sorrows have brought you to this moment in time?

Who grew the food that you've eaten so far today? Who transported it and sold it? Who made the clothes that you are wearing or built the building that you are sitting in? Our lives are so connected.

None of us really exists apart.

Independent.

When I contemplate the image of Indra's net, I have a sense of what it would feel like to belong everywhere, no hidden corners of avoidance or estrangement. I have a sense of finding a home even in the unfamiliar, because fundamentally all is connected. I have a sense of being able to recognize an aspect of myself in all because that mutual recognition is the infinite reflection. It's the very fabric of existence. This is so different from the alienation, divisiveness, and othering of current times, where we look to an ever-narrowing tribalism to feel safe or a disembodied identification with an avatar somewhere to feel alive.

As we grow, we can see that no being, no moment, no occurrence is unworthy of our care and attention. We discover that what we yearn for is close at hand. Every moment of our lives expresses the truth when we know how to look. St. Augustine put it so well:

> If you are looking for something that is everywhere, you don't need travel to get there. You need love.

TAKING CARE OF ONE ANOTHER

THE LAST CLASS I taught where I was physically present with a group before such gatherings were shut down was in early March 2020. No one really understood much other than that things were scary, people were getting sick, and hand sanitizer was at a premium. I was sitting in the audience, waiting to be introduced so I could go on the stage and begin teaching. The woman sitting next to me was phenomenally anxious, not unreasonably. "I wasn't sure whether to come," she began. "I'm not sure about anything. I'm just so anxious all the time."

"Well," I responded, "there are these breathing techniques where your out-breath is longer than your in-breath [see page 119] that can work to calm your nervous system so that it's easier to face a scary situation."

She wasn't interested in trying that.

"Well," I said, "there is lovingkindness meditation, which helps us feel connected to others and can help us be less scared."

She wasn't interested in that either.

On a wild intuition, I asked her, "Is there anyone you can help?"

To my surprise, she became radiant. "I do have an elderly neighbor. Maybe I can slip a note under her door and see if I can go get her groceries or something."

Look at that! I rejoiced within.

※

When we connect with others, we don't lose ourselves, we find ourselves. We find the voice within that isn't overcome by fear (though that may be in the room) or by unworthiness (though that may be there, too). We find the voice born of recognizing a bigger sense of possibility, which urges us to engage without the certainty of definite, immediate reward. We find the dimensions of what we consider a meaningful life. This is what gets us out of bed, out of lethargy, to see if life can be different. Connecting to one another is the dynamism that reminds us continually to affirm what might yet be rather than allowing discouragement or anxiety to lay waste to any sense of that vision. We are after all capable of not only the greatest wrongs but also the highest good. Many days, we face the direct question of what will get us to try to reach for the highest.

I read a news story that I thought of over and over again throughout the turbulence, uncertainty, and heartbreak of 2020, about when Sanford Middle School in Minneapolis launched a food drive to distribute to their students, people in the community, and really, anyone who needed help. They were filling food kits with staples like cereal, bread, and apples, as well as diapers, detergent, and other essentials. The original request was for enough to fill about 85 kits. As word spread, they anticipated enough for about 150 kits. On the day, donations kept coming and coming. And coming. There were miles of cars waiting to drop off food. People walked as well, carrying groceries in their hands. By the end of the day, an estimated 30,000 kits were delivered.

Similarly, my friend Shelly Tygielski, whom I first quoted in chapter 5, founded a mutual aid organization at the beginning of COVID called Pandemic of Love. She started with two Google Docs, one saying, *Get help,* the other, *Give help. Get help* was meant for people who, given the conditions of the virus and lockdown, needed help paying for rent, or utilities, or clothes for their children.

Shelly began pairing those requests with offers and then stepped out of the way of the match so that there was human-to-human contact, and relationships began to grow along with the offers. At the time of this writing, two years later, this grassroots, volunteer-led organization (or sort of non-organization, as we're used to defining them) had facilitated over two million matches around the world, with more than $60 million exchanged, and a great many connections established and flourishing. The friendships created are genuine, as people get to know and care for one another.

Also, at the time of my writing, Shelly was pairing up Pandemic of Love with people on the ground in Eastern Europe, offering support to families and children displaced from Ukraine, currently suffering a heartbreaking state of war, with massive dislocation and suffering. If you recall the quotation from Rabbi Nachman in the first chapter—"The Exodus from Egypt occurs in every human being, in every era, in every year, and in every day"—you get a sense of the quality of awareness that can see the devastation in Ukraine and understand that on a deeper level, it is not just "far away, over there, nothing to do with me."

✳

The world I believe is possible is one where we don't wake up and hear our neighbor is hungry and pull the covers up over our heads, roll over, and go back to sleep. Where we see countless people driven into homelessness, and don't reach uneasily for any silencing distraction, but continue to pay attention, as difficult as that might be. Most days, disconnection and strife seem to rule. But still, that heartbeat of connection is discernible when we learn to get a little quieter and listen for it. We can take that sense of life into our everyday encounters and situations. Based on interconnection, we respond with much more empathy, compassion, and a realistic sense of the world and how much we need each other. Interconnection enables us to see that what we do matters, because that action ripples out along these threads of connection. What we care about matters and who we are matters, because we are part of a greater whole.

Anne Lamott, the prolific San Francisco Bay Area novelist and activist, told me about using this story when she teaches Sunday school classes:

> There's a little girl, really struggling to fall asleep, really, really afraid and anxious, which is me. She keeps calling out for her mom to come into her bedroom in the dark. And the mom keeps coming in. In the first few times, she's very patient. "Oh, you're okay. Jesus is right here with you on the bed. You're fine. Just close your eyes and go to sleep now." And by about the fourth time, the mother's

getting impatient and exhausted. And she says a little harshly, "Jesus is right here with you on the bed, in the room, and you don't have to be afraid of anything and you can just drift off."

And the little girl says plaintively, "I need someone with skin on."

My understanding is that simple. All I know of God is Jesus and Mary, who I adore. I don't see how you can't. The message is, to me on a daily basis, get thirsty people water, teach little kids how to swim, and be God with skin. And for everyone I meet—whether it's a brand-new sober person or whether it's a very, very aged and lonely person in line at Whole Foods who everyone's avoiding because he or she may pull coupons out of their bag in the express line—I can be God with skin on and sit there patiently and smile and compliment them on what a really great hat they have. I keep it very simple.

That sense of purpose in life gives us a path. We might fall down, or get distracted, or meander awhile on a side street, or forget and be quite lost for a bit, but no matter what:

We have a path we can follow to a life that is less disconnected, much happier, and much freer.

That's the most important thing of all.

8

WITH THE LIGHT
OF CLARITY

✳

IN VARIOUS SCHOOLS of Buddhist teaching, the true nature
of the mind is described as free, unconfined, expansive—like
the sky. Its spaciousness is immense, unspoiled by the cloud for-
mations or storms moving through it, inclusive and open throughout anything.

It would be easy to imagine vast space as being vacuous, blank.
With our minds, though, just as light permeates the sky, the true

nature of our minds is permeated by the light of awareness. That inner light manifests as clarity.

So much gets illuminated as we pay attention with less distraction, fewer preconceptions, more willingness to come close to our experience. We can not only *inhabit* our lives more freely (enjoy our cup of coffee, for example, because we are actually present for it, not lost in multitasking), we can *understand* our lives more fully: What brings us suffering? What releases us from suffering? When are we strong? How alone are we, really?

All along the way of this journey we encounter questions like:

"What do I most deeply want?"

"What would I benefit from letting go of?"

"What do I believe is possible for me, for life?"

"What are the forces of constraint and restriction I can work through?"

We are not engaging in relentless, dismal self-scrutiny. And we are not dismayed if we don't have immediate answers. Being willing to ask the question is what's important.

We look at these questions with a lot of joy at our ability to make choices, to venture into terrain described by theologian Howard Thurman when he said, "Don't ask yourself what the world needs. Ask yourself what makes you come alive, and go do that, because what the world needs is people who have come alive."

Over time, we recognize the patterns that dampen that feeling of coming alive, and we work to loosen the threads they're woven of. We go through times when our perspective dramatically shifts, when our assumptions are deeply challenged, when we see new possibilities or sense that what has held us back from freedom or creativity or new ventures could actually be left behind. We have adventures. We experiment with different choices and resolutions.

And we come to intuitive insights into what actually brings us deeper happiness. We see possibilities for change that ignite a tremendous sense of aliveness.

In the description of insights that are classically born of meditation practice, one is known as *knowledge and vision of what is path and what is not-path*. What should we trust? What can we rely on? Within the context of formal meditation, this insight is a reminder not to be distracted by shiny things—by bright lights or lovely visions—but to keep practicing by paying attention, being mindful, until we are abiding in equanimity or peace. Don't settle for low-hanging fruit. Those experiences, like all experiences, come and go, and are exciting and lovely, but also beside the point of being free.

The true transformation comes within us, with how we approach everything—pleasant, painful, or neutral. It comes from what is born of connection, of openness. It comes from what is molded from the material that life presents us. We learn we can be steadier, more centered, more attuned, more loving, no matter what is going on. And we see that we can learn from our mistakes, rather than considering ourselves irredeemable and calling ourselves utter failures for not executing something perfectly. This, too, in life is a point where we can discern what is the path (everything is something we can learn from) and what is not the path (the opposite).

I'm applying that phrase—knowledge and vision of what is path and what is not-path—because I find it especially relevant in the context of fully living our lives. We can rely not on rigid opinion or belief but rather on clarity itself to recognize certain impulses and emotions: "I've been down this road before. This resentment / grasping / endless self-criticism is wrapped in such shiny paper, but I've seen its ultimate bitter unfolding. I think I'll let it go."

We might start in darkness and encounter the need to step into the unknown again and again, but over time, clarity about where suffering lies and where freedom lies dawns, to accompany us throughout the ups and downs of the journey.

In the light of clarity, we can ask ourselves, "In my family, what is the price of belonging? In my circle of friends? In my community?"

Sometimes that price is denying our genuine reactions or our discontent. Sometimes, it is never talking about something. Many of us can relate to this story I heard where a woman, knowing about her father-in-law's past prodigious drinking, asked her mother-in-law if he was drinking again. Her reply was "Not to speak of," which I take as a literal "Hush . . . don't go there."

We can ask ourselves, "What is the price of fulfilling this dream? What would I be compromising? What might I risk losing? What is the path and what is not the path?" Does it ask too much of us or too little, or is it looking more and more like a cul-de-sac? We bring together a willingness to open, a commitment to honesty, and the dawn of clear seeing, allowing us to walk an authentic path to greater happiness. We can walk it as who we truly are.

WHAT CHANGES IN OUR LIVES AS CLARITY DAWNS?

First off, we destigmatize pain

bell hooks once said that "one of the mighty illusions that is constructed in the dailiness of life in our culture is that all pain is a negation of worthiness, that the real chosen people, the real worthy people, are the people that are most free from pain."

I woke up the other morning thinking about a friend of mine, recalling how he took care of his partner until he died during the terrible early days of the AIDS crisis. I thought of how that experience marks the contours of his sorrow still, how he stepped up into compassionate care while in unimaginable pain, how this pandemic has seeped into that one for him. And I thought of the many people who are caregivers, and those who have recently experienced loss, and those who struggle accepting help, and those who feel ashamed when not in control. Life can be very hard.

I've been struck for a long time at the cruelty of a society that ties being frightened or confused or different or not being able to afford something with humiliation, as though your very life was worth less than another's. And yet, there is a whole other perspective we can have. I'm reminded of what Parker Palmer, the educator we met in chapter 3, says about autumn. Despite the fact that autumn is a time when nature sows seeds,

> I am rarely aware that seeds are being planted. Instead, my mind is on the fact that the green growth of summer is browning and beginning to die. My delight in the autumn colors is always tinged with melancholy, a sense of impending loss that is only heightened by the beauty all around.... I feel the power of metaphor.... I am easily fixated on surface appearances—on the decline of meaning, the decay of relationships, the death of a work.
>
> And yet, if I look more deeply, I may see the myriad possibilities being planted to bear fruit in some season yet to come.

In retrospect, I can see in my own life what I could not see at the time—how the job I lost helped me find work I needed to do, how the "road closed" sign turned me toward terrain I needed to travel, how losses that felt irredeemable forced me to discern meanings I needed to know. On the surface, it seemed that life was lessening, but silently and lavishly the seeds of new life were always being sown. . . .

Autumn constantly reminds me that my daily dyings are necessary precursors to new life. If I try to "make" a life that defies the diminishments of autumn, the life I end up with will be artificial, at best, and utterly colorless as well. But when I yield to the endless interplay of living and dying, dying and living, the life I am given will be real and colorful, fruitful and whole.

We are kind to ourselves as we journey

Taking the perspective Parker offers and making it real is essentially about kindness—kindness for ourselves, as well as for others. Clarity brings us to this because directly seeing the power and grace of kindness is one of the greatest myth-busting exercises we can engage in. Kindness is not a weakness or a secondary virtue, as we may have been taught for many years. It is not about giving in, or smiling weakly, or attempting to please everyone.

Not buying into that humiliation model when you're frightened or lonely or don't have enough money for some luxury is a good first step in kindness toward yourself, and that is radical. Seeing our troubling or contracted reactions like fear or craving simply as signs of suffering, rather than as something bad or weak, is applying kindness toward yourself. Remembering the natural interplay between darkness and light, the fragility of life circumstances and the possibility of accessing a hidden wholeness, is to practice kindness toward all.

> *This kindness, in itself, is a means of awakening the spark of love within you and helping others to discover that spark within themselves.*
>
> —TSOKNYI RINPOCHE

The poet Diego Perez goes by the name Yung Pueblo because, he says, it serves to "remind him of his Ecuadorian roots, his experiences in activism, and that the collective of humanity is in the midst of important growth." The practice of vipassana meditation has been a special inspiration for his work. Here is what he said to me about finding gentleness *within* that became gentleness *without* as well:

Before I started meditating, my heart felt so rough. It felt so rough and full. I wasn't a particularly bad person, but my interactions always felt like I could just be so much gentler. It wasn't until meditation taught me how to deal with myself gently that I was then able to bring that gentleness into my everyday affairs with my family, with my wife, with my friends. In a big way, I think meditating just helps me integrate this idea of gentleness, because you don't know what people are going through, you don't know what's happened to them or why they can be mean to you. But if you're able to maintain some degree of equanimity and some degree of lovingkindness toward them, at the very least, it'll protect your inner peace.

In the course of our lives, upsetting bits of memory, feeling, and impression get magnetized and begin to fasten together. Eventually, we have a clump of blocked energy, held-in passion for life, ready assumptions about our failures and our unworthiness. We start to react to events that are not actually connected to how we were hurt or disappointed or frightened to begin with, but somehow for us they seem to be. This is commonly called *trauma*. As Kimberly Ann Johnson says in *Call of the Wild:*

> Trauma narrows our vision, limits our options, shrinks our capacity, and gets us stuck fixating on ourselves rather than seeing the big picture. . . .
>
> Trauma is also not one thing. We tend to think of trauma as a specific event—like a car accident or a death or an abusive relationship—but it's not the events themselves that are traumatic. It's the way that we metabolize the events, or don't, that determines whether they linger in our system as unprocessed material causing record skips and literal or metaphorical indigestion.

Steve Dansiger is a onetime musician who eventually needed to become sober. He earned his doctorate in clinical psychology and became a licensed therapist. He developed the MET(T)A Protocol, a design for mental health agency treatment using Buddhist Mindfulness and EMDR (eye movement desensitization and reprocessing) therapy. EMDR encourages patients to briefly focus on a trauma memory while simultaneously experiencing bilateral stimulation, usually eye movements or back-and-forth tapping. (This is associated with a reduction in the vividness and emotion associated with the trauma memories.) EMDR is used in trauma and addiction treatment centers across the country and around the world. Steve, who has written extensively about trauma and twelve-step treatment, talked with me about how trauma can re-inflict trauma sufferers:

When someone who has unhealed, unprocessed, maladap-tively stored traumas encounters a new event that has some of the flavor, the sounds, the sights, the affect, the perspec-tive of the old event, it then turns it into this new, in-the-moment, terrible event. Without a narrative, without a time stamp.

If that doesn't get processed correctly, it reinforces the old stuff. The old stuff is killing me in the moment, and the things that don't get processed correctly in the moment re-inforce the knowledge of the system. It's like, "Yeah, it's bad, and it's never going to get good, and we need to always pro-tect ourselves." There's either the hypervigilance, "I'm going to look for that everywhere, all the time." Or "Nothing hap-pened," or "This drink will make sure that I don't think that anything really happened." It continues. All of it is designed to help me survive. I'm adapting to trauma. Unfortunately, it just starts this train in motion that ends up going against survival.

When I asked Steve to talk to me about how people respond to treatment for trauma using EMDR therapy, he said:

When you ask many of the people who come to the end of reprocessing, "What are you noticing now?" they'll say something to the effect of, "It's like a black-and-white picture. It's about five feet away. I totally see that it's me. I know that it happened, and I can see that it was awful, but it doesn't hold charge anymore."

Things that are not traumatic to us go through an innate adaptive process of moving to long-term memory found in the neocortical regions. This is where we have our ability to make meaning and to have executive functioning and all those wonderful things. The reprocessing just finishes that job for the memories that never made it through.

Steve's description of the black-and-white photo reminded me of something Sylvia Boorstein told me. Sylvia describes herself as a recovering catastrophizer. Anxiety is her default energy. "When in doubt, worry," she says. "If there is the slightest ambiguity, worry. I phone my son and he doesn't answer. The worst must have happened. Now there could be a thousand reasons he is not answering the phone. He's in the shower. He fell in love. He's sleeping. But my mind goes to the worst extrapolation of that. Anxiety is the free-floating hyperactivity of the mind that only tends to consider the worst possible outcome."

Sylvia first got involved in meditation practice to try to heal the effects of such continual anxiety—on her body, emotions, and relationships. Mindfulness works to give us some space from our thoughts so that we can choose whether we will take them to heart or let them go—at least until we can gather some more information. When the brain is spinning out one terrible outcome after another, it does not have enough space to clearly perceive the world around us as it is in this moment. Sylvia would be the first person to say she's wired in a way that predisposes her to anxiety. In her imagination, at any rate. She is not that way in the middle of an *actual* challenging circumstance, during which time she would describe herself as being as steady as a rock. She still may have some of the same kinds of thoughts, but she relates to them so differently that they can even be amusing. Just recently she said to me, "I have a new mantra." When I asked her what it was she was repeating to herself, she said, "Not every bus ends up in a ditch."

In looking at challenging tendencies, we're not trying to develop enmity toward anything, but rather we're coming to realize that we do have the capacity to process, get space from, understand, and integrate all of these experiences—however extreme.

When not integrated, we are in that state where we can easily be activated (common parlance is *triggered*, but I know several survivors of gun violence who have asked that we not use that word, so I try not to) and may act driven by that association.

In psychologist Tara Bennett-Goleman's book *Emotional Alchemy*, she details ten basic emotional patterns or schemas—ingrained patterns of perception that lead us over and over to react to similar activation with a painful, habitual set of thoughts, feelings, and reactions. The schemas she writes about include fear of abandonment, social exclusion (the feeling that we don't belong), and vulnerability (the feeling that some catastrophe will occur).

Though they may have helped us cope at the time we acquired them, they do not work so well for us now. Tara describes tools of mindfulness that directly help us transform these tendencies into wisdom and compassion. Several friends and I had fun the summer after the book came out, reading about the various schemas, discussing which was our predominant trait, reflecting on what was most difficult for us in others. We reminded one another to see whatever these were as forms of conditioning rather than a personal affliction or bad character trait.

It was fascinating for me to see how challenging I could find people who seemed to combine *unlovability* (a core feeling of being flawed) and *entitlement* (seeming to expect others to make up for it). That tended to awaken a sense of responsibility for fixing everything despite the sheer impossibility of that, and I'd feel trapped. Having that insight has been invaluable for me in understanding my conditioning.

We see that actions have consequences

Though the view should be as vast as the sky, keep
your conduct as fine as barley flour.

— PADMASAMBHAVA

As vast and open and free as our worldview may become, our actions—even seemingly small actions—can be finely and sensitively wrought, because they matter. What we care about matters. Where we put our energy matters. Erasing the divide between our espoused values and the intentions guiding our day-to-day actions matters. To enjoy integrity, we stop fragmenting and compartmentalizing our lives as much as we might tend to do. Telling lies at work each day and expecting great truths to descend in meditation practice on the weekend, for example, is pretty disjointed. Not impossible, perhaps, but talk about getting in your own way, or setting out to do something the hardest way possible! Why not give ourselves a break for once, and understand that all elements of our lives are intertwined.

Similarly, using our sexual energy in a way that is exploitative or harms ourselves or others, and then expecting to know transcendent love in a rarefied spiritual arena, is constructing a way forward strewn with complexity. Every aspect of our lives is connected to every other aspect of our lives. This truth is the basis for an awakened life.

We also need good boundaries, so as not to get lost in perfectionism, in endless, corrosive efforts to be in control of the unfolding of events, to make everything all better all the time. Those ideas do not reflect reality, and will lead inevitably to frustration and defeat. The core motivation that causes us to seek to bring our lives into alignment with how things are—joining discernment with our immense potential for happiness and connection—is love.

Omid Safi, the Sufi teacher we heard from in chapter 4, spoke with me of a connection between love and justice:

> In the Sufi tradition, love is the anchor. Love holds the center. Love is the ocean. Justice is like the different waves that may extend out of that ocean of love into the public arena. But it's got to come back to love. And I've definitely seen many cases in my own community and others where the work of justice is only fueled by outrage. That's okay. Because there's a lot of stuff you see around the world, including in our own communities, that if you're not outraged by, maybe you're not paying close enough attention.
>
> When that outrage turns into rage, you lose touch with the love that inspired you in the first place. My hope is that we can keep an open heart and a sense of curiosity about how that concern for the well-being and the well-doing of the planet can be grounded in love. I hope we can make room for a kind of justice practice, where the goal is the dignity and the well-being of all of us, including those who right now find themselves on the wrong side of history.

We can understand the real-life consequences of being lost in a chronically contracted state, as compared to the consequences of being more open and inquiring. When I mentioned this notion to Omid, he responded:

> It sounds like what you're saying is that in order for us to learn lessons about our own life, it calls for a personal reckoning, an examination and an exploration of what has unfolded in our own life and in our own journey. I do worry, though, that the pace of life is so intense, so all-consuming, that the insistence on having those spaces for inner exploration is a very countercultural move these days.

And yet, we find ourselves in need of that kind of understanding, perhaps now more than ever. That may mean going against the tide, going toward the more expansive, the more loving, with more presence in order to make that possible. During our conversation, Omid offered a wonderful bit of wisdom about presence:

> There's an eleventh-century Persian Sufi named Hujwiri (a.k.a. Hojviri) who has this wonderful practice. It's so simple to say, yet challenging to live and come back to. He just says, "Have your heart be where your feet are." It's so easy for us to either project ourselves into the future, or to think about all the things we hope will happen, or all the things that we might be afraid will happen, or to dwell on the past, than to think about all the things that hurt us or maybe some sweet memories in the past. And we're basically everywhere, except the here and the now. But the work can only be done in the here and the now.

How can this whole world of experience arise, yet there be nothing that can be held on to? How can the entire universe appear, only to vanish?

It's common to fall into one of two extreme views about reality. One of these extreme views tells us that there is something solid or secure or substantial to be found somewhere in this world of presentation, of seeing and hearing and smelling and tasting and touching and knowing through emotion and imagery and ideas. When we are caught or lost in this view, we grasp and cling to a world of change and appearance, and because of that discordance, we suffer.

The other of the extreme views tells us that nothing at all matters—that everything is a kind of void or blank, that we live in random, hopeless chaos. This nihilistic view leads to immobilization. It is the worldview within which we say, "Since everything is empty, insubstantial, what difference does anything make anyway? Why do anything?" This kind of preoccupation doesn't offer a full picture of life, because no matter what, there is conditionality in this world, interconnection, relatedness. Caring and love still matter.

I feel like the conditioning of my childhood and the general infrastructure of society is toward the former: hold on tight, try to seize control, accumulate a lot of stuff to deny change. You'll feel safe that way; you'll be invincible that way. The waves of the other extreme view are also strong these days, many would say especially among younger people. Cynicism over leadership, despair over climate change, and hopelessness over having any effect on the intransigence of systems all can lead to exhaustion and the hollow conviction that there's nothing that can be done.

The Middle Way avoids both these extreme views. We neither

take it all to be inherently solid, nor do we take it that nothing matters. We emerge into that very delicate place in between where everything arises, yet has no substance. The world is shimmering, it's translucent, it's all happening; yet everything is insubstantial, fleeting, evanescent. One never excludes the other. They are like the two wings of a bird.

It is hard for words to precisely convey this point of meeting. The Buddha often used images to try to convey some of this sense of all appearances arising, with nothing we can hold on to. He said life is like:

a rainbow,

an echo,

a dream,

a drop of dew on a blade of grass,

a flash of lightning in a summer sky.

What does a deeper glimpse into this truth of change offer us, ultimately? We see that there is a tender, exultant beauty to every hour, in fact to every minute we have just because we are alive. Yet at the same time, everything we hear and see and feel and want and know is fleeting, ungraspable. The fragility and dynamism of life is also what makes it so vital. Every experience, every encounter, every realized desire, and every unfulfilled longing that comes into our lives is moving, changing. Our everyday reality is as insubstantial and shimmering as light ... and in its very presence, miraculous. It is hard for words to convey both our ability to rejoice at the wondrousness of life as it continually flows into being and the poignancy forged in the insubstantiality of constant change as it all continually recedes.

Life is short, and it is sacred.

We live in an intricate, extraordinary, ephemeral world—all transparent and transitory, like a rainbow, like an echo, like a drop of dew on a blade of grass, like a flash of lightning in a summer sky. It's a world of joyous birth and renewal, and of an unremitting need to let go. It is a world of great loss and also one of so much possibility. Ultimately, it is a world where we experience nonseparation from life's essential openness.

We see we can break the mold

I stayed in my friend's apartment in New York City for a while, more than twenty years ago, while she was on a meditation retreat. I was working on a book that came to be called *Faith*, and I was mesmerized by a saying my friend had posted over her desk. I've been mesmerized by the saying ever since. The funny thing is that I don't think I remember it quite right, but it has somehow described both my pull to and my fear of writing since I first saw it. The saying as I remember it was "Scare me. Tell me the forbidden story."

"I'd really rather not" is my usual first response when I think of it. "Let's go somewhere more decorous, more mannered, more predictable." But of course the original advice, even if I conjured it from the ether, is more to the point.

Some form of that advice can be found offered by highly creative people, like novelist Dorothy Allison: "Write the story that you were always afraid to tell. I swear to you that there is magic in it."

Or writer and showrunner Michaela Coel: "Write the tale that scares you, that makes you feel uncertain, that isn't comfortable. I dare you."

No matter what story the world has told us we must claim as ours, if we are willing to step out of that box, with openness, a spirit of discovery, and awareness we see that we can be free. We can decide on how we want to tell our own story.

As Joél Leon, whom we met in chapter 6, tweeted recently:

Your resume gets to change. Your story gets to shift. Your title gets to expand. Your role gets to pivot. Your definition of "success" doesn't have to be linear. Our dreams get to be as big as our imaginations . . . our greatest tool as humans is our ability to reimagine the story laid bare in front of us—what will the next chapter in this magical life of yours be?

Yung Pueblo, the poet we met earlier in this chapter, spoke to me of how creativity emerges as a force of change, both personally and beyond:

When people move together in mass movements, that really changes history. But what's going to make that work even stronger is the individual work we do to find our own healing tools, our development of our personal happiness of letting go of all the past wounds or the heaviness we're carrying and just figuring out a way to allow more clarity and creativity and joy to emerge from our minds.

Right now, I'm just focusing on writing, but I definitely see how it's a critical component in making change, because we have to be able to imagine things differently and imagine in bigger ways if we're going to actually make tangible material change. That's why I have shifted my role as an active organizer to being a full-time writer, trying to help people imagine that they can actually heal themselves and that they can take that healing to better communicate with each other and love each other better.

One thing I keep observing over and over is that when the mind is so dense with conditioning, it keeps multiplying. You keep reacting and adding to that density. When you reverse that process and you start pulling back all those layers and unbinding all these knots in the mind, you get a natural emergence of creativity that comes out of nowhere. It doesn't necessarily mean that everyone becomes an artist, but there's a new creativity you can use to look at old problems in your life and come up with new solutions.

The process of going deep within to access and then express the truth we find is the greatest of creative endeavors, whether it is formally recognized as art or not. Every conversation, every encounter, every working through of a misunderstanding, and every new unfolding in a friendship is an outlet for that process. In that way, our lives themselves become our creative medium, and our days are marked by discovery, celebration, and surprise.

In a way, we take ourselves less seriously. While still maintaining standards of excellence, we can nonetheless relax more, surrender more to seeing what happens next. We can enjoy the unruly process of getting somewhere, as well as hold in high regard the idea of the "somewhere."

We become less afraid of making mistakes as well—not because we've become reckless or cavalier but because we've glimpsed the immensity of the space beyond the nine dots in the exercise

Jon Kabat-Zinn showed me (see chapter 1, page 20). We've inherited the limited arena of the nine dots. It is conventional and expected. But we can come to trust the immensity beyond it, and we have—or at least we can find—the courage to venture there.

That process won't yield a flawless result every time, but it will allow us to sense the infinite potential in new places, in new beginnings. After all, the work of *creating* isn't the same as the work of *replicating*. Creating is a state of being fully open, fully alive. As Shakespeare wrote, "To unpathed waters, undreamed shores."

✳

Or as James Lapine, longtime collaborator of the late composer and lyricist Stephen Sondheim, wrote in their musical *Sunday in the Park with George* of the artist Georges Seurat:

> White
> A blank page or canvas
> His favorite
> So many possibilities

9

ASPIRATION

※

S PRING 2021 came around, and there I was in Massachusetts, still sheltering in place. I watched *Saturday Night Seder* online once again for Passover. I appreciate it so much I think I'll watch it every year as long as it's available on YouTube, whether or not it is my only Seder.

As many know, a Seder ceremony ends on a note of aspiration, with the heartfelt, cell-deep yearning to be free, expressed as "Next year in Jerusalem." As I noted in the first chapter, I am not referring to a physical location or the heart-wrenching geopolitics associated with the term. Jerusalem has long been a widely used metaphor, drawn on by people ranging from poet William Blake to singer-songwriter Rufus Wainwright. I use the word *Jerusalem* as the symbol of escape from "narrow straits"—freedom from confinement due to being stuck, due to not questioning the prevailing story being told about us by others or the prevailing story we're telling ourselves, due to confusion about how to be different, how to be fully ourselves. We need courage and imagination to take that first step in the dark to find a new way to live. The fuel for that is aspiration.

If I were trying to describe myself in one word at age eighteen, it would have been *fragmented*. I kept looking for a narrative thread to tie the slices of my life experience into something meaningful, something that could be onward leading. There was something within me that flickered, undying and undeniable, saying that wholeness and connection were possible, that things could be different and I could be happier. That formed into an aspiration to bring that possibility to life, to make it real, and so I went to India to learn how to meditate.

Many of us experience ourselves as fragmented, perhaps as confident and funny when we are with our friends but much more hesitant and unsure when we are at work. Perhaps we take risks when we are with others, but are timid when alone, or are cozily comfortable when alone, yet are painfully shy and withdrawn when with others. Or maybe we tend to drift along with the tides of circumstance, going up and down, not knowing what we might really care about more than anything else, but thinking there must be *something*.

Aspiration captures that *something*. And aspiration powers the journey to making that *something* real, living it more fully. Aspiration takes us from a more abstract or distant appreciation of a dream to stepping right into the center of possibility and change.

Aspiration is different from corrective goals or expectations, though there might be any number of those we would find healing or exhilarating to resolve. For example, I have a friend who has long loved singing. Sadly, when he was in third grade, the singing teacher told him his voice was bad and to just mouth the words. Maybe he didn't have the most beautiful voice in the world, but really!

One year, when my friend was well into adulthood, someone gifted him with a series of singing lessons ... not to improve pitch or key but to help release him from that awful comment. Sure enough, he worked through some things and is now known to belt out songs on lots of different occasions. His friends might tease, "He's no Pavarotti" (well, neither am I), but it makes him quite happy to sing, and it actually makes the people around him quite happy to hear him sing because of his evident joy. It was a nice knot to disentangle.

There might be any number of specific aspects of life it could be good to adjust, but if those changes don't come to pass in the way we imagine, we can readily adapt. Those adjustments are not going to define our deepest sense of what our lives are about. Fulfilling them might be nice or therapeutic, but not fulfilling them won't make it any less possible to have a fully lived, deeply connected life.

I'm afraid of heights, for example, and have been for years, ever since a near fall off a cliff on Maui. I recently saw a film made about Tibetan teachers Tsoknyi Rinpoche and Mingyur Rinpoche's journey to their birthplace in remote Nepal: a village called Nubri.

Friends who also watched it kept writing me saying, "What an incredible landscape . . . Look at their wide and delighted smiles . . . Wouldn't it be amazing to do that trek someday?"

As for me, I couldn't take my eyes off those narrow, eroding, washed-out-looking paths, with drops of what seemed like a million miles if your foot slipped. People living in the distant villages they passed through appeared ecstatic at the chance for teachings. No one looked happier than I was, though, when they boarded a helicopter for their return trip. Maybe this is something I can get over in this lifetime; maybe not. Except for feeling uneasy at mezzanine seating in a theater and a determination that I will never visit that cliff on the way to Nubri, it doesn't really affect my life.

Aspiration is not the same as a bucket list, that compilation of sparkling possibilities we would like to experience before we die. These, too, might be rewarding or exciting yet aren't necessarily core to our vision of what's truly meaningful in life. A few years ago, I realized that I had met the amazing people I'd hoped someday to meet, and I had actually completed my bucket list. I went to my friend Joseph Goldstein and asked, "I finished my bucket list. Do you think I'm going to die?" He looked at me somewhat puzzled and responded, "Just make another list."

※

Aspiration is bigger than realizing a specific, narrow hope or dream and vanquishing fears around it. It's a broad vision of meaning in one's life, a North Star by which to navigate, a guide to returning when you've felt lost. Even though an aspiration is overarching, it's not hovering somewhere overhead, disconnected from everyday life. Aspiration does manifest through our intentions, through the ways we speak or act or we hold back from speaking or acting, through our choices every day. Aspiration is an active presence in our lives every day that we recall it, we reflect on it, we work with it.

My own aspiration is to live in touch with goodness. I aspire to be a force of goodness, to weave a story of life not made of fear but of love. I aspire to truly "walk my talk" in the matter of love, a quality so easy to speak about or extol but so often hard to make real.

Interestingly, of the projects I thought I might try to accomplish back at the beginning of pandemic isolation, I regrettably didn't learn Spanish, and in terms of thoroughly cleaning out my house, I will quote someone I heard on TV, whose name I didn't catch: "I always thought that if I only had the time, I'd thoroughly clean out my house. Turns out time wasn't the problem." What did become more vibrant and alive for me while we were getting through a situation I would never have chosen was resolving to be kinder. That meant everything from rereading emails before pressing Send (to decide if I wanted to change anything to avoid misunderstandings) to making a point of thanking people whose kindness and generosity it would have been easy to take for granted.

I could see how having a clear aspiration gave me ballast in a world of constant change, a reservoir of heartfulness to infuse my choices, my relationships, and my reactions. I see now how aspiration illuminates each crossroads we come to.

Many of us long for an underlying sense of meaning, something we can still believe in no matter what happens to us, a navigational force to pull all the disparate pieces of our lives together into some kind of whole. A commitment to an aspiration like kindness can be the thread that twines throughout our various successes, disappointments, delights, and difficulties—making our lives seamless.

In 1997, while attending a conference in San Francisco called Peacemaking: The Power of Nonviolence, I walked by the writer Alice Walker, who was having an informal conversation with a group of people. I overheard her say, "As I get older, I realize that the thing I value the most is good-heartedness." Her comment was my big takeaway from that conference.

I often just sit and reflect on that comment. To explore good-heartedness as the thread of meaning in one's life means examining if we can be *strong* and still be *kind*, be *smart* and still be *generous*. It means exploring whether we can be profoundly compassionate to ourselves and at the same time intensely dedicated to compassion for those around us. To place goodness as central in our hearts can also mean being something of a rebel. What you feel gives your life more of a direction and meaning can be seen by others as a little mawkish or pretentious. Do we trust it nonetheless?

Can you give voice to *your* deepest aspiration?

Take some time to look at it, maybe gently expand it as you explore it.

Take some time to celebrate that aspiration. It can light up your life.

SATURDAY NIGHT SEDER

LET'S RETURN to the *Saturday Night Seder* program, where we began. There is a wonderful series of aspirations expressed at the very end of this Seder, with personal interpretations of the classic saying "Next year in Jerusalem." From actor and playwright Harvey Fierstein:

> Next Year in Jerusalem, to me means, next year we will be in our home. And that home will be a world without fear, a world without hunger, a world without poverty and rot.
>
> Next year, we will be in a world that is caring and supportive of its inhabitants,

and a world where its inhabitants are caring and supportive of the world in which they live.

Next year we will look to our great minds for leadership,

and eschew loudmouth fools.

Next year we will remember the lessons of kindness
from our youth.

Next year we will aspire to live our possibilities.

Next year we will be grateful for the gift of life we've
been given.

Next year we will achieve our goals and share our
bounty with family, friends, and neighbors.

Next year the word *stranger* will be meaningless because next year, we will all be together in our home.

So

Next Year

in Jerusalem.

May we continue this journey toward freedom together.

May our actions redound to the welfare and happiness of all
beings.

May wisdom and compassion grow.

May peace be born anew and soon prevail.

ACKNOWLEDGMENTS

✳

I'd like to thank Bob Miller and everyone I have worked with at Flatiron for caring about their authors; my agent, Joy Harris, for being the super ally that she is; all those who model this journey and who gave me permission to quote their written work or our podcasts together; the very skilled Barry Boyce for developmental editing; Ariel Bushnell and Hannah Dubner for comprehensive research; and Lily Cushman for holding the whole scene together. You all made it so much easier, more interesting, and more fun.

APPENDIX

✳

THE EIGHTFOLD PATH (SEE CHAPTER 1)

Right View or Understanding—Developing a greater awareness of sources of suffering in our lives, sources of release from suffering, and aspects of reality that help us live differently, such as the understanding that actions have consequences.

Right Intention—Cultivating thoughts and intentions based on non-harming, letting go of grasping, and strengthening lovingkindness.

Right Speech—When speaking, we aim for speech that is truthful, helpful, kind, and timed wisely.

Right Action—Acting in ways that do not cause harm, such as not taking life, not stealing, and not engaging in sexual misconduct, so as to deepen peace within oneself and harmony in one's community.

Right Livelihood—Making an ethically sound living; being honest in business dealings.

Right Effort—Practicing letting go of thoughts and feelings that create suffering for ourselves and others, and cultivating those that foster connection, wisdom, and true happiness for ourselves and others.

Right Mindfulness—Practicing mindfulness of one's body, feelings, mind, and mental qualities.

Right Concentration—Developing the ability to focus our attention steadily in a wholesome way, without filters of grasping or aversion.

We begin with right view, but every step we take along the way enhances and deepens this sense of right view, which is where we started. Hence, the "Eightfold Dot" (see page 26).

MEDITATION GUIDE

How to Use This Guide

If you are reading this rather than listening to it, it would be useful to take a moment to think through how you're going to use this guide. With written guidance, I find it helpful to read the introductory information a few times, then focus on a particular instruction. If you are looking at lovingkindness meditation, for example, perhaps choose one recipient for a session, such as yourself or a benefactor, rather than trying to do it all at once from the beginning. Over time, it will be a lot easier to broaden the lovingkindness instruction to include several categories of recipients in one session.

I'd also invite you to keep the instructions nearby as you sit. If you feel uncertain or confused, you can always open your eyes, take another look, and begin again.

Getting Started: Posture and Timing

Begin by sitting comfortably. You don't have to be in an uncomfortable or unfamiliar posture. You can set the time you plan to sit for, using an app or an alarm. If you are new to meditation, five to ten minutes is a fine period to experiment with. If you are more experienced, you might still choose to do five to ten minutes or extend it to twenty minutes or whatever you feel comfortable with.

You can close your eyes if you feel comfortable, or if you are accustomed to meditating with your eyes open, that's fine. And if you get really sleepy, it's a good idea to open your eyes and just continue on with the practice.

Letting Go of Distractions and Returning to the Original Object to Begin Again

There are many possible objects of attention for meditation. Some exercises use the breath, some a mantra or saying, some use a sound, some use other sensations in your body, some use phrases of lovingkindness. In this exercise, we'll use the breath as our chosen object. As my early meditation teachers would say, *You don't have to believe in anything in order to feel your breath. If you are breathing, you can be meditating.* The point of this practice is not *stopping our thoughts* but learning to change our relationship to them. Your breath can serve as the vehicle for coming back to yourself.

We're going to sit together resting our attention on the feeling of the breath. The operative word really is *rest*. We might believe, "If I get a death grip on the breath, my mind won't wander," but it will actually wander more. The breath is like home base. I can virtually guarantee that it's not going to be nine hundred breaths before your mind wanders. Maybe it will be two. Maybe it will be one, maybe five, but probably, pretty quickly your attention will wander—your attention jumps to the past, jumps to the future, judgment, speculation, something. And then comes the magic moment, when you realize, "Oh! It's been quite some time since I last felt a breath!" That's the moment when you have the chance to be really different. So instead of judging yourself or comparing yourself or calling yourself a failure, see if you can *gently* let go, and with kindness toward yourself, return your attention to the feeling of the breath. If you have to do that over and over again in the course of the session, that's okay.

Starting the Breath Meditation

To begin, sit comfortably, as comfortably as you can. As I said previously, you can close your eyes or not, however you feel most at ease. We actually start with listening to sound. It's a way of relaxing deep inside, allowing our experience to come and go. Of course, we like certain sounds and don't like others, but we don't have to chase after them to hold on or push away—just let them come, let them go.

Now bring your attention to the feeling of your body sitting, whatever sensations are most prominent.

Bring your attention to your hands and see if you can make the shift from the more conceptual level—like *fingers*—to the world of direct sensation. Sensing any pulsing, throbbing, pressure—whatever it might be. You don't have to name these things, but feel them.

Now bring your attention to the feeling of your breath, the actual sensation of your in- and out-breath. Wherever you feel it most distinctly— maybe that's the nostrils or the chest or the abdomen. You can find that place where the breath feels strongest. Bring your attention there and just rest. See if you can feel one breath.

If you like, you can use a quiet mental notation like *in, out* or *rising, falling* to help support your awareness of the breath, but very quietly, so your attention is really going toward feeling the breath. One breath at a time.

If you find your attention has wandered, you've gotten lost in thought, spun out in a fantasy, or you fall asleep . . . Truly, don't worry about it. See if you can let go gently and bring your attention back to the feeling of the breath.

And when you feel ready, you can open your eyes or lift your gaze and conclude the meditation.

Using Sound as the Object

This is a good meditation in and of itself and also serves as a good alternative to the breath if for physical reasons, like asthma, or for emotional reasons that affect your breathing, you find settling your attention on the breath more unsettling than settling. The skill set is very similar, in that we have a chosen object, our attention wanders, and when we realize it, we practice letting go and returning to the chosen object.

One of the ways this meditation is used is to show us that we can actually meet any experience with greater clarity, openness, spaciousness, kindness. Even as we like certain sounds and we don't like others, we don't have to chase after them, to hold on or push away, fretfully trying to seize control over that which we will never have control over. Some beautiful, wonderful sounds arise; others are quite unpleasant or jangly. Unless you're responsible for responding to the sound, this is a time when you can actually practice simply being present. Noticing the sound for what it is, you don't have to elaborate, "Oh, that's a bus. I wonder what the bus route is. Maybe they should change the bus route so it's more convenient for me." But simply hear.

To begin with, you can take a comfortable posture and recognize that sound is continually coming and going outside of our control. In this meditation, you can close your eyes or keep them open. If your eyes are open, you can find a spot in front of you to just rest your gaze. Let it go. And hear the sounds that arise and pass away as though they're washing through you. There's nothing you need to do about them, you don't need to respond, you needn't try to stop them; you don't even have to understand them. Whether it's the sound of my voice or other sounds, some near, some far, some welcome, some not so welcome. Maybe it's the sound of traffic or the wind rustling through the trees. In either case, it's simply sound rising and passing away. You can notice changes in intensity, in volume, as the sound washes through you, without interference, without judgment. You don't have to send your ears out to listen. Relax deep inside, create a vast sense of space in which sound is rising and falling, rising and falling.

If you find yourself getting tense in reaction to a sound, take a deep breath, just relax. If you find yourself craving more of a sound, here, too, you can simply relax. Because the sound will rise and pass away without regard to our clinging or condemning. Simply notice that sound rises, we have a certain response to it, and there's a little space in between those two. And stay open for the appearance of the next sound.

And when you feel ready, you can open your eyes or lift your gaze and relax.

Introducing Lovingkindness

Lovingkindness meditation begins with a suggestion to sit comfortably, relax, relax physically, relax emotionally. This isn't a practice where we strive to make something special happen, or seek to fabricate a state, or manufacture anything, but rather we get in touch with a more natural space within us. So our posture reflects that relaxation.

With each person or each category of being, see if you can bring an image of them to mind or feel their presence as though they were sitting right in front of you. Say their name to yourself and offer the phrases of lovingkindness to them, focusing on just one phrase at a time. Gather all your energy, all your attention, to say that one phrase. Don't struggle to fabricate or manufacture a feeling or a sentiment. Just relax deep inside, let the power of intention, which is the practice of lovingkindness, lead the way. And whenever you find that your mind has wandered, your attention has wandered, simply begin again.

1. Choose the three or four phrases that express what you most deeply wish for yourself (and ultimately for others) and begin to repeat them silently.

2. Repeat the phrases, like "May I be happy . . . ," with enough space and enough silence so that it is a rhythm that's pleasing to you. I have a friend who thought he'd get extra credit for saying more phrases—you don't need to be in a rush. Gather all your attention around one phrase at a time.

3. I want to emphasize again that you don't need to manufacture or fabricate a special feeling. The power of the practice comes from our full, wholehearted presence behind each phrase, from being willing to pay attention to ourselves and others in truthful, though perhaps unaccustomed, ways. If you fear sentimentality or phoniness, this is an especially important reminder.

4. This practice is different from affirmations that tell us we are getting better and better, or insist that we're perfect just as we are. If it feels phony or like you are begging or imploring ("May I *please, please* be happy already") remind yourself that it is a practice of generosity—you are giving yourself and others a gift of loving attention.

5. You may decide it is helpful to coordinate these phrases with the breath or simply have your mind rest in the phrases.

6. When you notice your attention has wandered, see if you can let go of the distraction gently and return to the repetition of the phrases. Don't worry if it happens frequently.

Choosing Phrases to Recite Silently

Traditional phrases include:

"May I be safe."

"May I be happy."

"May I be healthy."

"May I live with ease."

That last phrase means "May the elements of daily life, like work and family, relationships, go easily, not be such a struggle."

"May I be safe. May I be happy. May I be healthy. May I live with ease." You can use these phrases or any others that are more personally meaningful to you.

The feeling tone is not one of asking or beseeching but one of gift giving. It's an offering, a blessing. It is likened to handing someone a birthday card and saying, "May you have a great year." Similarly, we say, "May you be happy." Or, "May I be happy."

When I do this practice, I tend to say the full phrase only the first time in the sequence, "May I be safe. Be happy. Be healthy. Live with ease." But that's really up to you. Feel free to experiment.

Lovingkindness Toward Ourselves

You can close your eyes if you feel comfortable; if you are accustomed to meditating with your eyes open, that's fine. And if you get really sleepy, it's a good idea to open your eyes and just continue with the practice.

We begin by actively taking delight in our own goodness. So much of our time can be spent remembering the mistakes we've made, our negative actions. Here, we counteract that. We actually consciously point our attention toward something good we've done. It may be a very small thing, but bring it to mind. And if no particular action comes up, think of a good quality that is alive within you. We do this not to be egotistical or conceited but to rejoice in the potential for goodness we all share in.

We then silently repeat phrases that reflect what we would wish most deeply for ourselves, not just for today but in an enduring way. Phrases that are big enough, that are general enough, so that it can represent a gift we would give to ourselves and also ultimately to all of life. This is what we would wish for all beings everywhere, beginning with ourselves.

Common phrases include: "May I be safe. Be happy. Be healthy. Live with ease." You can use these phrases or any others that are more personally meaningful to you. Just gather all your attention behind one phrase at a time, as though you were planting a seed in the ground, and then let it go. "May I be safe. Be happy. Be healthy. Live with ease."

Whenever you find your attention has wandered away from the phrases, gently begin again. No matter where your mind has gone, no matter how far away it has wandered, it doesn't matter. You can actively practice kindness in that moment. Gently let go, gather your energy together, begin again. You can find a rhythm that's pleasing to you, with enough space and enough silence so that the phrases are emerging from your heart. "May I be safe. Be happy. Be healthy. Live with ease." Or whatever phrases you may be using.

Now visualize yourself sitting in the center of a circle. The circle is made up of the most loving beings you've encountered in this life, or maybe you've never met them, but they've inspired you in some way.

Perhaps they exist in current time; maybe they've existed historically or even mythically. That's the circle. It's like a circle of love, loving energy. There you are in the center. You can experience what it's like to be the recipient of that quality of attention, of care, as you gently stay in touch and repeat the phrases of lovingkindness for yourself. You might change the phrasing as though the phrases are coming *from* them *for* you, "May you be safe, be happy, be healthy, live with ease."

Many, many emotions may arise. You may feel joyous, you may feel grateful, you may feel embarrassed, like you'd just like to duck down and have them each offer lovingkindness to one another, forgetting about you. Whatever emotion it is, you can let it come and let it pass as though it were washing through you. The touchstone is the repetition of the phrases. And here, too, whenever you find your attention wandering, it's fine. That is the magic moment of the meditation. We practice letting go, we practice beginning again.

"May I be safe. Be happy. Be healthy. Live with ease."

We can search the entire universe for someone who is more deserving of our love and affection than we are ourselves, and we won't find that person anywhere. We ourselves deserve our own love and affection more than anybody. So as you receive this energy coming toward you, be in touch with that truth. It's okay to want to be happy, to be safe. Our wish is that all beings, including ourselves, be happy, be safe.

And then to close the session, you can let go of the visualization, dissolve the circle. Keep repeating the phrases of lovingkindness for a few more minutes. You're making the offering at the same time that you are receiving the energy.

For all the time we usually spend judging ourselves, putting ourselves down, we are recapturing that energy, that force. Let it fill your body. Let it fill your being.

And when you feel ready, you can open your eyes or lift your gaze. Pay attention to whatever effect the meditation may have had and notice throughout the day whatever effect it may be cultivating, what may be enduring.

Lovingkindness for a Benefactor

Call to mind someone who's helped you, been good to you, or kind to you, or maybe you've never met them, but they've inspired you. If someone like that comes to mind, bring them here. You can get an image of them, say their name to yourself, get a feeling for their presence, and offer the phrases of lovingkindness to them. Wishing for them just what it is you've wished for yourself. "May you be safe. Be happy. Be healthy. Live with ease." Even if the words don't fit totally, it doesn't matter; they're the conduits of your heart, they're the vehicle for connection. "May you be safe. Be happy. Be healthy. Live with ease."

You might choose an adult, a child, a pet . . . Who lifts your spirits? Who has you smiling when you think of them?

You can let thoughts, emotions, memories, arise and pass away, without clinging to them, without condemning them. Maybe you have the thought *What does she need me for? She's so great* or *What does he need me for? He's so great.* Or *You know, I thought they were really there for me, but there was that one time . . .*

Just let those thoughts come and go. Your attention can steady on the repetition of the phrases.

If you find yourself weaving a story, see if you can let it go and gather all your attention behind one phrase at a time. "May you be safe. Be happy. Be healthy. Live with ease." Or whatever your phrases are.

You might recall the help they have given you or the lift they bring to your spirits if the practice starts seeming mechanical . . . then wholeheartedly gather your attention behind one phrase at a time.

As you close the session, feel what it is like to acknowledge those who bring you joy instead of taking them for granted, and see if you can bring some of that into your day.

Meditation on Sympathetic Joy: Lovingkindness for a Friend Who Is Doing Well

What is essential to develop in terms of oneself are the abilities to rejoice and to have gratitude. Now bring to mind a pleasurable experience you had recently, one that carries a positive emotion such as happiness, joy, comfort, contentment, or gratitude. Maybe it was a wonderful meal, or a reviving cup of coffee, or time spent with your kids. Perhaps there's something in your life you feel especially grateful for—a friend who is always there for you, a pet excited to see you, a gorgeous sunset, a moment of quiet.

If you can't think of a positive experience, be aware of giving yourself the gift of time to do this practice now.

Take a moment to cherish whatever image comes to mind with the recollection of the pleasurable experience. See what it feels like to sit with this recollection. Where in your body do you feel sensations arising? What are they? How do they change? Focus your attention on the part of your body where those sensations are the strongest. Stay with the awareness of your bodily sensations and your relationship to them, opening up to them and accepting them.

Practice inviting in the feelings of joy or delight and allowing yourself to make space for them. Acknowledge and fully experience such emotions.

From this greater state of inner sufficiency, we will offer lovingkindness to someone whom we care about; someone it is easy to rejoice for. It may be somewhat difficult even then, but we tend to more easily feel joy for someone on the basis of our love and friendship. Choose a friend and focus on a particular gain or source of joy in this person's life. Do not look for absolute, perfect happiness in their life, because you may not find it. Whatever good fortune or happiness of theirs comes to your mind, take delight in it with the phrases of lovingkindness: "May you be safe. Be happy. Be healthy. Live with ease." If you prefer, you can switch to a phrase of sympathetic joy, like "May your happiness not diminish."

Even if jealousy or annoyance should arise, be kind to yourself, and noticing how confining and painful they feel, see if you can let go gently and return to the phrases. If needed, you can always go back to the reflection on the good you experience.

When you feel ready, you can open your eyes or lift your gaze and end the session. See if you can notice the feelings of resenting or enjoying someone else's good fortune as you go through your day. And remember, we all can choose where to put our energy.

Compassion Meditation: Lovingkindness for a Friend Who Is Having Difficulty

In doing meditation specifically designed to nurture compassion, we can use the lovingkindness phrases we have been using, or as an alternative, you might choose to repeat just one or two phrases, such as "May you be free of suffering" or "May you find peace." It is important that the phrase be meaningful to you. Sometimes people feel more comfortable using a phrase that implies the wish for a more loving acceptance of pain, rather than *freedom from pain*. You should experiment with different phrases, seeing which ones support a compassionate opening to pain and which ones seem to lead you more in the direction of aversion or grief.

The first recipient of the compassion meditation is a friend who is struggling right now in some way. Perhaps they seem to feel lost or alone. This should be a real person, not just a symbolic aggregate of the difficulties in life. Spend some time directing the lovingkindness phrases—"May you be safe. Be happy. Be healthy. Live with ease"—or whatever phrases you have been using toward this person. Or experiment with using a specific compassion phrase.

If you feel yourself moving from the trembling of the heart that is compassion into states of fear, despair, or sorrow, first of all, accept that this is natural. Breathe softly, and use your awareness of the breath to anchor yourself in this moment. Reach underneath the fear or rejection of pain to the sense of oneness that underlies it. You can reflect on that sense of oneness and rejoice in it.

You can repeat the lovingkindness phrases for a friend who is struggling right now. "May you be safe. Be happy. Be healthy. Live with ease." Or simply choose a phrase of compassion, like, "May you be free."

Now think of a strength your friend has—maybe a sense of humor or kindness toward others. Perhaps a source of resilience or a specific action where they cared about someone else. Bring a greater fullness of awareness of them as a person larger than just their difficulty or challenge. Offer lovingkindness to that person represented in the larger view.

And for the last few minutes of this sitting, you can be spontaneous: just see who comes to mind, someone you care about deeply, someone you have difficulty with, a stranger, someone you just met. Allow them to arise in your awareness one at a time and make the offering of lovingkindness to them, people, animals, whoever it might be.

And when you feel ready, you can open your eyes or lift your gaze and end the session.

Lovingkindness for a Neutral Person

A neutral person, the person we don't strongly like or dislike, is often someone who plays a role in our lives—say, someone who works in a store we go to, who may be the kind of person we normally look right through or ignore. We're going to see what happens when we hold them in our hearts and wish them well.

Begin with two reflections:

All beings want to be happy.

All beings are vulnerable to change, to loss.

And begin the offering of lovingkindness to yourself. "May I be safe. Be happy. Be healthy. Live with ease." Repeat the phrases with enough space and enough silence so that it's pleasing to you. Gather all your attention behind one phrase at a time. If you find your attention wandering, don't worry about it. You can simply let go and begin again.

"May I be safe. Be happy. Be healthy. Live with ease." Feelings may come and go, memories may come and go . . . allow them to arise and pass away. Here the touchstone is the repetition of the phrases. You don't have to block anything else and you don't have to follow after it. "May I be safe. Be happy. Be healthy. Live with ease."

Call to mind a friend, the first friend who comes up for you. See if you can get an image of them, say their name to yourself, get a feeling for their presence, and offer the phrases of lovingkindness to them. Even if the words don't seem perfect, that's okay. They're the vehicle for the heart's energy, so they're serving us.

Call to mind someone you might encounter now and then, a neighbor, a checkout person at the supermarket, someone you don't really know, perhaps you don't even know their name, the first person like that who comes to mind. And bring them here, even not knowing their story, you can know that they want to be happy just as you do, that they're vulnerable to pain or loss just as you are, and you can wish them well. "May you be safe. Be happy. Be healthy. Live with ease."

We'll finish the meditation by offering lovingkindness in a spontaneous way to anyone who comes to mind, different people, animals, those whom we like, those whom we don't like so much—in a bold expanse of our own power of the heart. "May all beings be safe. Be happy. Be healthy. Live with ease."

Lovingkindness for a Difficult Person

Let's sit together. You can have your body at ease. See if your back can be straight without being strained. Close your eyes or not, whatever you feel most comfortable with. You could begin with the offering of lovingkindness to yourself and the silent repetition of the phrases that are meaningful to you, phrases like "May I be safe. Be happy. Be healthy.

Live with ease." The skill set is when you find your attention wandering, you get lost in thoughts, spun out in a fantasy, if you fall asleep, really, don't worry about it. See if you can let go gently. Turn your attention to the repetition of the phrases.

Let's see if a mildly difficult person comes to mind, perhaps not starting with the person who's hurt you the most in this life or in your eyes has behaved just so horribly on the world stage, just somebody with whom there's a little bit of resentment or dislike or fear.

If someone like that comes to mind, you can bring them here. Get an image of them or say their name to yourself. Get a feeling for their presence and just see what happens as you offer the phrases of lovingkindness to them.

It's common to feel resentment and anger, even toward a mildly difficult person, but we undertake this practice in a spirit of adventure. What happens when instead of going over and over our old grievance, we pay attention to this person in a different way, wishing they could be free of some of the suffering that binds them, wishing they themselves could be filled with the spirit of lovingkindness and compassion?

In the case of more grievous injury or pain, you may find you need to change the phrases. You can start out with these, and if it's a struggle in any way, see if there's something else you could repeat. For example, I've had one student say in terms of someone else, the most he could actually be repeating, "May you be free of hatred," and that worked. "May you be filled with lovingkindness. May you find clarity and well-being." (After all, they would be less difficult if they themselves were happier!)

There's a lot of room for creativity in this practice. Start out with the phrases you've been using. See what happens. Remember you're not trying to manufacture any emotion or feeling. And if you feel swamped or strained, then go back to simply offering lovingkindness to yourself. Think of yourself as deserving of love and care, and generate the phrases for yourself. It's never wrong to do that.

And we experiment, in a kind of active imagination: Is there a way you can visualize this person that makes it easier? Like on a desert island with no boat, no aqueduct, no tunnel? They have food (you're not trying to starve them) but no way at all of coming closer?

We'll finish the meditation by offering lovingkindness in a spontaneous way to anyone who comes to mind, different people, animals, those whom we like, those whom we don't like so much, in a bold expanse of our own power of the heart. "May all beings be safe. Be happy. Be healthy. Live with ease." When you feel ready, you can open your eyes, lift your gaze. See if you can bring some of this energy to different encounters throughout the day.

Lovingkindness for All Beings

As you sit, relax, close your eyes, or have them slightly open.

See what categories come to mind, those beings who have a home and those who don't, those who are waking up, who are awake in the literal sense, those who are asleep right now—whatever pairs of opposites or complementary sets come to mind, being sure to include all aspects of the whole.

Gently repeat the phrases, focusing all your attention on one phrase at a time. If there are no waves of emotion or sentiment, don't worry about it. The power of the practice is developed through the power of concentration, so gather all your energy behind just one phrase. And if you find your attention has wandered, see if you can let go of the distraction without judgment and come back to repeating the phrases. "May you be safe. Be happy. Be healthy. Live with ease."

We then move on to offer the phrases of lovingkindness to *all beings everywhere, without distinction, without exception, without separation*. This is an expression of our capacity to connect to and care for all of life, so open your heart, and begin with the phrase "May all beings": "May all beings be safe. Be happy. Be healthy. Live with ease." All beings, then all creatures, all individuals, all those in existence. Each way of phrasing the immensity of life opens us. We connect to the boundlessness of life, so many life-forms.

We offer lovingkindness to all beings, all creatures, all those in existence stretching infinitely in front of us without boundary, and to either side.

All beings, all forms of life behind us, and to either side.

Those above, and those below. "May all beings everywhere be safe. Be happy. Be healthy. Live with ease."

And when you feel ready, you can open your eyes or lift your gaze.

Notice if the sense of spaciousness, expansiveness, lovingkindness, affects you throughout the day.

ABOUT THE AUTHOR

✳

Sharon Salzberg is a meditation pioneer, world-renowned teacher, and a *New York Times* bestselling author. She was one of the first to bring mindfulness and lovingkindness meditation to mainstream American culture more than forty-five years ago, inspiring generations of meditation teachers and wellness influencers. Sharon is cofounder of the Insight Meditation Society in Barre, Massachusetts, and the author of twelve books, including the *New York Times* bestseller *Real Happiness*, now in its second edition, and her seminal work, *Lovingkindness*. Her podcast, *The Metta Hour*, has amassed six million downloads and features interviews with thought leaders from the mindfulness movement and beyond.